A WALK THR

The Doctors of the Church

by

Sister M. Cecilia Bush, C.S.J.

The Spiritual Life Center
7100 East 45th Street North
Wichita, Kansas 67226

✝Eugene J. Gerber, D.D.
Bishop of Wichita
February 28,2001

Copyright ©2001, Catholic Diocese of Wichita
All rights reserved.

Library of Congress Control Number: 2002102771
ISBN: 0-9718195-0-5

Supporters for the publication and exhibition projects:
Tony and Sherry Catanese
Jerome Gerber
Paul and Ann Konecny
Larry and Wah-leeta Steckline

Icons of the thirty-three Doctors of the Church, painted by Ann Torrini of St. Louis, Missouri, were a gift to the Catholic Diocese of Wichita by the Bob and Helen Bergkamp family. The icons are on exhibition at:
The Spiritual Life Center
7100 East 45th Street North
Wichita, Kansas 67226

This book is available at special quantity discounts when purchased in bulk for educational purposes. To purchase additional copies of this book or for information regarding this project write or call:
The Spiritual Life Center
7100 East 45th Street North
Wichita, Kansas 67226
(316) 744-0167

First printing January 2002
Printed in the United States by Mennonite Press Inc., Newton, Kansas

TABLE OF CONTENTS

Foreword v

Introduction vi

PART I—The Long Century, 325 to 451 A.D.
The Church Embattled by Heresy

Saint Athanasius, Father of Orthodoxy 3

Saint Hilary of Poitiers,
    Doctor of the Divinity of Christ 5

Saint Ephrem the Syrian,
    Doctor of the Universe and Marian Doctor 8

Saint Basil the Great, Doctor of Monasticism 10

Saint Gregory Nazianzen,
    Champion of the Nicene Creed 13

Saint Cyril of Jerusalem, Author of Catecheses 15

Saint Jerome, Doctor of Biblical Science 18

Saint John Chrysostom, Doctor of the Eucharist 20

Saint Ambrose, Doctor of Virginity 23

Saint Augustine of Hippo, Doctor of Grace 25

Saint Cyril of Alexandria,
    Doctor of the Incarnation 28

Saint Peter Chrysologus,
    Advocate of Papal Authority 30

Saint Leo the Great,
    Doctor of the Unity of the Church 33

PART II—The Middle Ages, 500 to 1500 A.D.

Saint Gregory the Great,
    Servant of the Servants of God 36

Saint Isidore of Seville,
    Guardian of the Liberal Arts 38

Saint Bede the Venerable,
    Last of the Latin Fathers 41
Saint John Damascene, Doctor of the Incarnation ... 43
Saint Peter Damian, Reformer and Diplomat 45
Saint Anselm of Canterbury,
    Father of Scholasticism 48
Saint Bernard of Clairvaux,
    The Mellifluous Doctor 50
Saint Anthony of Padua, The Evangelical Doctor 52
Saint Albert the Great, The Universal Doctor 55
Saint Thomas Aquinas, The Angelic Doctor 57
Saint Bonaventure, The Seraphic Doctor 59
Saint Catherine of Siena,
    Spiritual Mother and Papal Advisor 62

PART III—Post-Reformation Defenders of the Faith, Sixteenth and Seventeenth Centuries

Saint Peter Canisius, Second Apostle of Germany ... 66
Saint Robert Bellarmine,
    Champion of Church and State Relations 68
Saint Lawrence of Brindisi,
    Capuchin, Polemicist, Diplomat 70

PART IV—Doctors of the Great Love of God, Sixteenth through Nineteenth Centuries

Saint Teresa of Avila, Doctor of Prayer 74
Saint John of the Cross,
    Doctor of Mystical Theology 76
Saint Francis de Sales,
    Evangelist and Spiritual Father 78
Saint Alphonsus Liguori,
    Founder of the Redemptorists 81
Saint Therese of Lisieux,
    The Little Flower of Jesus 83

FOREWORD

Usually when one wishes to read about the Doctors of the Church, one finds them in the midst of other historic figures of the Church. Rarely can you find a presentation solely on the thirty-three Doctors. Sister Cecilia Bush, CSJ, has provided just such a presentation. Each Doctor is presented in brief with basic contextual information and highlights of their contribution to the Church

This work will be appreciated by ordinary readers and scholars as well. Sister Cecilia avoids the complexities of the various theological controversies and opts instead for a more general summation of the key insights and concerns. An avid historian will certainly wish to turn to additional sources to provide the historical details that cannot possibly be part of this concise work.

A unique feature of this work is the final paragraph for each Doctor, which presents some reference concerning the Blessed Virgin Mary. This along with the prayer given with each Doctor's story allows for a devotional dimension to this work. The faithful may then be drawn to give thanks to God for each Saint's contribution to the proper reverence due Our Blessed Mother.

Through the wisdom of the Saints, God has provided His people with rich food for mind and heart. We know He will continue to do so. May God reward Sister Cecilia for making available to us these literary portraits of the Doctors of the Church.

✝Eugene J. Gerber
Bishop Emeritus of Wichita

INTRODUCTION

The Doctors of the Church are visible signs that God keeps His promises. He promised that the gates of hell would not prevail against His Church; and in times of crisis, He raises up defenders of the faith, whenever fundamental doctrines of the Church are under attack. God also promised that He would be with us always; and He sends men and women whose lives and writings deepen our understanding of the faith and enliven our desire for deeper union with God. These providential people, who combine great sanctity with eminent learning, are proclaimed by a Pope or an ecumenical council as Doctors of the Church.

The Age of Martyrs

The first three centuries of Christianity are called the Age of Martyrs, during which the Church underwent ten persecutions and thousands died for the faith. But as Tertullian remarked, the blood of martyrs was the seed of Christians and the Church continued to grow. "Afflict us, torment us, crucify us, in proportion as we are mowed down, we increase," he said. During this time, the guide of faith was the Apostles' Creed, which stated the faith but did not explain it. This led to misinterpretations which came to a head in the fourth century.

The Long Century:
The Church Embattled by Heresy

No longer persecuted from without, the Church found its enemies from within and underwent some of its greatest threats in what is known as the Long Century, dating from 325 A.D., the Council of Nicaea, to 451 A.D., the Council of Chalcedon. It has been said that so much of Catholic belief was confirmed during these 126 years that no serious student of Church history can fail to concentrate on the Long Century (Wuerl 1982, 84-5). At first the Church faced the threat of Arianism, which denied the Divinity of Christ. Later heresies are called the Christological Controversies, because they denied that Jesus was one Person with two natures-human and divine. Divine Providence raised up thirteen of the 33 Doctors of the Church as champions of the true faith during this critical period.

The Middle Ages
500-1500 A.D.

Twelve servants of God, who lived during the long period called the Middle Ages, from 500 to 1500 A.D., have been proclaimed Doctors of the Church. Their example and writings have added to the rich heritage of the Church and have endured down through the centuries because of their great value to theological and human knowledge. Not only did their works clarify and develop Christian doctrine but they also preserved all existing secular knowledge from destruction by the barbarian invaders during the Dark Ages. Major contributions to theology and philosophy were made during the thirteenth century with the development of Scholasticism by St. Albert the Great and St. Thomas Aquinas.

Post-Reformation
Defenders of the Faith

So great was the challenge to the survival of the Church from the sixteenth century Protestant Revolt that the fact that it emerged from this major crisis renewed is positive proof of its divine institution. Among the many remarkable people whom God raised up to defend the Church at that critical time, three have been proclaimed as Doctors of the Church. They not only preached against the reformers but sought to bring about the changes needed within the Church. They pointed out that it was not the Catholic religion that needed reformation but rather the people who professed that faith who needed to change. Thus, they led the Catholic Reformation against the Protestant Revolt.

Doctors of the Great Love of God

The lives and writings of five Doctors of the Church provide deeper knowledge of the intimate union with God which is possible for the faithful. They are visible signs that God's promise to remain with us always is meant to be a personal sharing in our daily lives. They have left the Church models of different types of spirituality.

A Walk Through History With The Doctors of the Church

PART I

The Long Century

325 A.D. The Council of Nicaea to
451 A.D. The Council of Chalcedon

The Church Embattled by Heresy

Saint Athanasius
Father of Orthodoxy, c. 295-373

Saint Athanasius is called the Father of Ortho-
doxy because, as the dominant opponent of
Arianism, he formulated our belief in the
Blessed Trinity. Born in Alexandria, Egypt, around 295,
he was ordained a deacon in 318 and accompanied
Bishop Alexander to the Council of Nicaea in 325. The
Emperor Constantine had called this Council to settle
a controversy between Alexander and Arius, a priest of
his diocese. Arius taught that only the Father was God.
Since the Son was "begotten" by the Father, He was the
Son of God only by adoption. Last of all on this triad
was the Holy Spirit, who Arius taught, was inferior to
both, since He proceeded from the Father through the
Son.

Although the Council decreed that the Son was
coequal to and of the same substance as the Father, the
worst of the struggle had just begun. When Athanasius
became bishop of Alexandria in 328 and proceeded to
promulgate the Council decrees, he became the target
of the Arians against whom all his writings were
directed. From then on, the history of Arianism became
the history of Athanasius, who insisted that the Father,
Son and Holy Spirit had the same divine nature through
eternal generation.

Ordered by the Emperor to admit Arius to Communion, he refused and was exiled to Trier, Germany, in 335.
Recalled by Constantine II in 337, he was then deposed
by the Arian bishops and replaced by George the
Cappadocian, an Arian. After George died, Athanasius
again returned to his see for about ten years. But for
almost two generations, Athanasius was abandoned in
his fight against Arianism, which continued to spread.
Things got worse in 350 when Constantius became sole

emperor and the heresy took root in Italy, Germany, and Western Europe. In 355, Constantius convoked a council at Milan and condemned Athanasius. When Pope Liberius refused to comply, the Emperor set up an anti-pope in Rome. By then Arianism had become so widespread that St. Jerome exclaimed, "The world groaned and was astonished to find itself Arian."

After another six years in exile in the Egyptian desert, during which he wrote some of his major works, Athanasius returned to seek unity in the Church but was again banished by the Emperor Julian, who wanted to restore paganism. Back during the short reign of Jovian, he was soon exiled for a fifth time, this time by the Emperor Valens, who favored Arianism. But such an outcry arose from his people that the order was rescinded in 364. Athanasius then spent the rest of his life consolidating the decrees of the Council of Nicaea and initiating action for the triumph of the Nicene Creed, which expanded the Apostles Creed to state: "We believe in one Lord, Jesus Christ, the only Son of God, eternally begotten of the Father, God from God, Light from Light, true God from true God, begotten not made, one in being with the Father."

Of Athanasius, his friend St. Gregory of Nazianzen said: "He was the true pillar of the Church...and his doctrine the rule of the orthodox faith." After innumerable combats for the ultimate victory of the true faith, Athanasius died in Alexandria in 373.

Athanasius and Mary

In defending the divinity of Christ, Athanasius contributed mightily to the theology of Mary. In his *Life of Antony*, he called her "God-bearer." He presented her as the model of virgins, and centered on her personality as a program of Christian perfection in his *Letter to the Virgins*. He cited Psalm 45:10-11 as proof of Mary's virginity and royal descent: "Hear, O daughter, and see and incline your ear, forget your father's house, because the King desired your beauty." Athanasius noted Mary's unique privileges by applying to her Psalm 87:5: "Mother of Sion shall say, a man, and a man begotten of her and the Most High Himself formed her" to be the mother of the God-man. (O'Carroll, 1982, 61-2)

Prayer

Father, as a true pillar of the Church, Saint Athanasius defended the divinity of Christ despite exile and persecution. May we treasure the true faith which he worked so diligently to preserve. We ask this through Christ the Lord. Amen.

Saint Hilary of Poitiers
Doctor of the Divinity of Christ, c.315-c.367

At first it seemed to be Athanasius against the world in the battle against Arianism. But eventually new champions of the faith began to spring up in many places. Emerging as the Athanasius of the West was Saint Hilary, bishop of Poitiers in France. He was ordained bishop around 353 when the heresy was at its height and was determined to stop the spread of Arianism in Western Europe.

Born in Poitiers around 315, he had married in early life and had a daughter Arba. He was converted by reading the Prologue to St. John's Gospel and hearing that the Word was made flesh thus making all children of God. When he refused to condemn St. Athanasius at the Council of Beziers in 356, he was exiled to Phrygia but continued to administer his see by correspondence. While in exile, he wrote two important works and became the first Latin writer to become thoroughly familiar with Greek theological writings.

His work *De Trinitate* (On the Trinity), the first Latin extensive study of the Blessed Trinity, affirmed that there were three distinct Persons in the Trinity, all with the same nature. He taught that the Trinity was fully revealed when the Son of God came to earth. Because his chief purpose was to prove the divinity of the Word Incarnate, Christ is the center of all his teaching.

The other work written during his exile was *De Synodis* (On the Synods), a historical treatise which included the many formulas of faith in the East and how they were to be interpreted. In this way, he tried to reconcile Eastern and Western thought and to clear up misunderstandings between Catholics and the moderate Arians.

Because the Eastern Arian bishops considered him a troublemaker, Hilary was allowed to return to his diocese in 361. His last days were spent in ministering to the spiritual needs of his people, in maintaining the integrity of the true faith and in bringing back those who had strayed. Since he had seen how effective they had been in spreading Arianism in the East, Hilary introduced the singing of hymns in Western Europe. He took the authority of the Church for granted because it represented unity in Christ. He always based his doctrine on Scripture.

Hilary stressed a simple faith leading to piety, understanding and knowledge. He also assisted St. Martin of Tours in spreading monasticism in Gaul. Outstanding for the firmness of his faith, Hilary preached, wrote and suffered in defense of the Divinity of Christ up to his death in Poitiers around 367.

Hilary and Mary

Saint Hilary of Poitiers interprets 1 Corinthians 15:47 as referring to the role of the Holy Spirit in Mary's conception of the God-Man. He says that "the first man is from earth, a thing of dust, the second man is from heaven...the child-bearing is from the Virgin and the conception from the Spirit." He depicts Joseph as a witness to the conception by the Holy Spirit because whenever Mary and Joseph are mentioned in the Gospels, she is called the Mother of Christ not the spouse of Joseph. Hilary affirms that Mary is the Mother of God by showing the identity of the Son of God and the Son of the Virgin. He said, "The only begotten Son of God taking the body of our nature from the Virgin." (O'Carroll, 171)

Prayer

Almighty and eternal God, Saint Hilary affirmed our faith in Three co-equal Divine Persons, each possessing the same nature. Grant that we may grow constantly in deeper devotion to this great mystery. We make our prayer through Christ our Lord. Amen.

Saint Ephrem the Syrian
Doctor of the Universe and Marian Doctor,
c.306-373

uite unique among the defenders of the faith in this period was St. Ephrem the Syrian, who preferred singing to argument. A deacon of Edessa in modern Turkey, he was given the title of Harp of the Holy Spirit because of his efforts to instruct and counteract heresy with original hymns and poems. Immensely prolific in sacred poetry, Ephrem was a contemplative who chose to sing to God rather than to study about Him in learned books. He gets much of the credit for introducing music into public worship.

Ephrem was born in Nisibis in Mesopotamia around 306 and headed the catechetical school there. Since he accompanied Bishop James to the Council of Nicaea in 325, he would become involved in the Arian controversy from its earliest stages. When Nisibis came under the control of the Persians, Ephrem migrated to Edessa, where he became a deacon and taught in the exegetical school, which he probably helped to found. Most of his extant works were written during this time.

All of his writings, even his controversial compositions against heretics and pagans, were mystical in nature. Even his sermons were composed in narrative verse for special feast days and were never surpassed for their ability to touch as well as to teach. His only prose works were commentaries which covered the whole Bible. His innumerable hymns, which both instructed and charmed, were an aid to piety and faith. Lyrical in style, they were meant to be sung in Church and are classified as exhortations to virtue, panegyrics on saints or mysteries and instructions against heresy. These hymns which added luster to Christian assemblies, were sung to the music of one Harmonius, who collaborated with Ephrem.

Ephrem's poems, hymns, and discourses are very important in the history of Catholic doctrine. He taught that the human person was made in the image of God by free will, domination over all creation, aptness to receive the gifts of God, and the facility with which the human mind can grasp knowledge. Ephrem believed that the Eucharistic consecration, the Incarnation and Redemption were all the work of the whole Trinity. He taught that the Trinity, especially the Holy Spirit, is involved in bringing Christ's glorified humanity under the Eucharistic species, and that through the Eucharist, the Holy Spirit abides in human hearts where He adapts Himself to their littleness. These thoughts helped in the discussions going on about the nature of our belief in the Trinity.

Ephrem's striking and clear description of the Last Judgment served as an inspiration for Dante. The Syrians devotedly call Ephrem Doctor of the Universe and Pillar of the Church.

Ephrem and Mary

Writing about Mary was one of Ephrem's favorite things. He stressed her virginity and held that she was a virgin before the birth of Jesus, during His birth and after His birth. Ephrem's belief in the Immaculate Conception was shown by his constant dwelling on Mary's sinlessness. To Ephrem, Mary was Mother of God. He asked, "What mother has ever called her son, Son of the Most High?" He is probably the first writer to call Mary the Bride of Christ. Ephrem also speaks of Mary as a symbol of the Church, which depends on her. In fact, Ephrem's voluminous writings on Mary prove that he deserves the title of Marian Doctor. (O'Carroll, 132-3)

Prayer

God of joy, your deacon Saint Ephrem sought to teach the faith and counteract heresy by means of hymns and poems. May we imitate him by striving to touch the hearts of others as we seek to enlighten their minds with eternal truths. We ask this through Christ Your Son. Amen.

Saint Basil the Great

Doctor of Monasticism, c.329-379

aint Basil the Great was one of the so-called Cappadocians, who sounded the death knell of Arianism even if he did not live to see its demise. Born in Caesarea around 329, Basil had it made spiritually, both by heredity and environment. His parents, Basil the Elder and Emmelia, were saints, as were his grandmother Macrina, his brothers, Gregory of Nyssa and Peter of Sebaste as well as his sister, Macrina the Younger. While studying in Constantinople and Athens, he was a classmate of Gregory Nazianzen and the future Emperor, Julian the Apostate. After being baptized, he founded a hermitage in Pontus in the Black Sea area. Ordained in 365, he returned to Caesarea and dedicated himself to defending the Council of Nicaea. He thus contributed greatly to the victory of belief in the Nicene Creed.

St. Basil wrote three books defending the divinity of Christ, which the Arians denied. In clarifying the doctrine of the Trinity, he has been called the Doctor of the Holy Spirit because of the defense of the divinity of the Third Person of the Blessed Trinity, which he presented in a small treatise called *On the Holy Spirit*. Besides many other works, he left behind numerous homilies and 365 letters which give valuable information on the history of the Church in his time. In all his writings and teaching, Basil depended on the Bible and was faithful in referring everything to it. He also was the first to stress the importance of unwritten tradition.

Basil is called the Doctor of Monasticism because he founded his own community and wrote several rules for monastic life. Saint Benedict was greatly influenced by these rules when founding his order. Basil based his concept of religious life on the perfect practice of the two great commandments of the Gospel rather than on the vows of poverty, chastity and obedience. The Liturgy of the Hours evolved from Basil's introduction of psalm-singing into public worship.

He excelled in his office as Bishop of Caesarea by frequently visiting his diocese, helping the poor, and instructing his flock through sermons, which rank as major theological works. Basil's formal declaration that the Holy Spirit is God, consubstantial with the Father and the Son, played a significant role in the decrees of the Council of Constantinople, held two years after his death. A great champion of Christian unity, his efforts to reunite people divided by a schism in Antioch also came to fruition after he died in 379. Basil was only 49 years old at the end but had completely worn himself out for the faith and the Church.

Basil and Mary

St. Basil, like St. Albert the Great and many other saints, referred to Mary under the title of prophetess, a person endowed with more than ordinary spiritual and moral insight and character. He believed that the Holy Spirit bestowed this name and title on Mary by saying: "I went to the prophetess." In this, Basil followed the teaching of Origen, who called Mary prophetess because of the *Magnificat*. In this context, Mary is acknowledged to have in still higher degree all the goodness and beauty which are found in all the other saints. Moreover, Basil believed that it was through her intercession that these saints have received their own great endowments. He also lauded Mary's humility, as the safe treasury of all virtues. (O'Carroll, 71)

Prayer

God our Father, St. Basil excelled in defense of the divinity of the Holy Spirit. Grant that we may be aware of the Spirit's presence in our souls and become ever more docile to His guidance. We ask this through Christ our Lord. Amen.

Saint Gregory Nazianzen
Champion of the Nicene Creed, c.330-c.390

W orking hand-in-hand with St. Basil, his long-time friend, was Saint Gregory Nazianzen. In one of his sermons, Gregory said: "Worship Him Who hung on the cross because of you, even if you are hanging there yourself." In his fight against Arianism, Gregory had ample opportunity to practice what he preached. Although he was attracted to life as a hermit, he was called to take active roles in the Church, which culminated in disappointments, controversies and seeming failure.

Born around 330 in Arianzus, Cappadocia (modern Turkey), into a family of saints, he was completing his education in Athens when he met St. Basil and joined him in a life of solitude in Pontus. Responding to the pleas of his father, St. Gregory Nazianzen the Elder, Bishop of Nazianzus, he returned home to assist him with Church and family matters. At that time, celibacy was not required of the clergy.

Terrified at priestly responsibilities after his father almost forcibly ordained him, Gregory fled into the desert for a time. Upon his return, he wrote such a profound treatise on the priesthood that it even influenced Saint Gregory the Great. At the insistence of Saint Basil, he was consecrated bishop of Sasima but never took possession of his see because of threats of violence if he did so.

In 378, the Catholics of Constantinople begged him to become their bishop and to restore the faith in their city, where most of the churches were Arian. Unable to be installed as bishop because of Arian persecution and betrayal of his friends, Gregory preached quietly in his Resurrection Chapel and contributed five very important sermons explaining the Nicene Creed and the Blessed Trinity. He clarified the concept of three distinct Persons, each divine, with each Person God in nature and substance. He taught that the Old Testament revealed the Father, the New Testament the Son, and that the Holy Spirit is fully revealed now "by making souls like God in baptism, which He could not have done if He were not God." Even Saint Jerome came to hear him.

When the Emperor Theodosius called the First Council of Constantinople in 381, Gregory presided and was said to be the keenest mind there. This Council affirmed that the Holy Spirit is coequal to the Father and the Son, and added to the Nicene Creed the words: "And in the Holy Spirit, the Lord and giver of life, who proceeds from the Father and the Son, with the Father and the Son He is worshiped and glorified. He has spoken through the prophets."

Gregory was confirmed as Bishop of Constantinople during this Council but never took possession of the see because opposition to his appointment divided the Church. Retiring to Nazianzen, he acted as bishop until he found a successor in 383 and then spent his life in prayer and study until his death in 390.

Besides 44 artistically perfect orations, Gregory left many letters, more than 16,000 lines of poetry of theological and historical nature and other works.

Gregory and Mary

Two generations before the Council of Ephesus, Gregory was calling Mary "*Theotokos*," Mother of God. "If anyone does not believe that Holy Mary is *Theotokos*, he is without the Godhead," he wrote. He called Mary the Temple of Christ and saw in her the beginning of virginity in the fullest sense. A teaching of Gregory shows the emergence of belief in Mary's Immaculate Conception from the fourth century and had great influence on Eastern thinking on this doctrine. "He took all things human save sin," Gregory said, "conceived of a virgin who had been purified previously by the Spirit in soul and body." (O'Carroll, 160)

Prayer

Merciful God, in a life marked by disappointment, controversy and seeming failure, Saint Gregory Nazianzen harmonized these trials with the joys yet to come. In our own difficulties, may we like Gregory unite ourselves with Jesus who hung on the cross for us. We make our prayer through Christ, Your Suffering Servant. Amen.

Saint Cyril of Jerusalem
Author of Catecheses, c.316-387

Saint Cyril of Jerusalem also played a major role in the Council of Constantinople. Like Saint Athanasius, Cyril spent 16 of his 35 years as bishop of Jerusalem in exile because of his defense of the Divinity of Christ against the Arian heretics.

He is believed to have been born in Jerusalem around 316 and to have died there in 387. In or after 342, he was ordained by Maximus, bishop of Jerusalem, whom he succeeded in 350. He is said to have been present at the Council of Tyre at which Saint Athanasius was deposed from the see of Alexandria because of his stand against Arianism and also at a council held in Jerusalem in 346, when Athanasius was reinstated.

As bishop of Jerusalem, Cyril fearlessly stood for the true faith. Although some of his adversaries stigmatized him as an Arian, Cyril never accepted any doctrine contrary to Orthodox Catholic teaching and sought for his diocese faith, law, order and peace. Driven from his see by Arian heretics in 357, he took refuge in Tarsus, where he became noted for his sermons which deeply touched the hearts of the people.

Reinstated in 359, he suffered another shorter exile in 361. Later at the command of the Emperor Valens, he was absent from his see from 367 to 378 but was cleared of all charges by Saint Gregory of Nyssa, the brother of Saint Basil.

Participating in the First Council of Constantinople in 381, Cyril accepted the term "consubstantial" to define the divine nature of all Three Persons of the Blessed Trinity. This Council showed the triumph of the true faith over Arianism. Some intransigent Arian Bishops were refused entrance to the Council. In fact, Arianism had been falling apart from within because of divisions about what they believed. Then after the heresy lost imperial support, it collapsed. The Emperor Theodosius made Catholicism the state religion and Arian bishops could no longer hold churches or ordain bishops.

Only one of Saint Cyril's sermons is extant. In it, he spoke of the healing of the paralytic in the manner of a contemplative exposition of Sacred Scripture and caught the authentic tone of the Fourth Gospel. But Cyril's reputation as a Doctor of the Church rests on the *Catecheses*, a series of Lenten pre-Baptismal instructional addresses for Sacramental preparation. The last five of these instructions are called the *Mystagogic* and were delivered to the newly baptized after Easter. These *Catecheses* are used today in the Rite of Christian Initiation of Adults (RCIA). They concern Baptism,

Confirmation, and Eucharist and are considered the richest document on the liturgy of the early Church. They authentically affirm the Holy Sacrifice of the Mass. By means of these instructions, believed to have been delivered in 346, Cyril took people from simple faith to a deeper knowledge based on Scripture and the Creed.

Cyril and Mary

Most of Saint Cyril's Marian doctrine is contained in *Catechesis XII*. He treated her virginal conception at length and showed that the word "father" applied to Joseph did not mean physical paternity. Although he used the word *"Theotokos"* only once, he staunchly affirmed Mary as Mother of God and called Jesus the Virgin-born God. God the Word was made man in truth, Cyril said, of the Virgin by the Holy Spirit, who sanctified her to receive the One through whom all things are made. On the Eve–Mary parallel, Cyril taught that since death came through the virgin Eve, there was need that from a virgin, life should appear. As the fallen angel in the form of a serpent deceived the one, so the Archangel Gabriel brought the Good News to the other, Cyril said. (O'Carroll, 114-5)

Prayer

God of truth, Your servant Cyril of Jerusalem presented profound mysteries in a clear and understandable manner. May we be led by his teaching from simple faith to firmly grounded knowledge of You. We ask this through our Lord Jesus Christ, Your Son, who lives and reigns with You and the Holy Spirit, one God, forever and ever. Amen.

Saint Jerome
Doctor of Biblical Science, c.345-420

nother Doctor of the Church who assisted at the First Council of Constantinople was Saint Jerome. He had gone to Constantinople in 380 to study under Saint Gregory Nazianzen. After the Council, he was summoned to Rome by Pope Damasus, who made Jerome his secretary and commissioned him to revise the translations of the New Testament and the Psalms. Thus began Jerome's monumental work in Sacred Scripture.

Jerome was born at Stridon in Dalmatia around 345 and educated in Rome, where as a youth he lived a worldly life but spent his Sundays exploring the Catacombs. After experiencing a change of heart, Jerome traveled to the East, visited holy people and settled as a hermit in the desert of Chalcis for prayer, study and penance. While there, he added Hebrew to the Latin and Greek, which he already knew, and was ordained a priest by Paulinus, Bishop of Antioch.

After he had been called back to Rome by the Pope, Jerome began to foster deep spirituality among certain Roman noble women, who were also well educated and were able to help him with his translations of Scripture. All kindness to his close associates, Jerome's sharp tongue and his manner of attacking abuses alienated many people. Because of continuing conflicts and criticism of his work as spiritual director of these noble women, Jerome left Rome in 385 and settled in Bethlehem. Saint Paula and her two daughters accompanied Jerome to the Holy Land, where combining Jerome's patrimony with financial help from Paula, they built a monastery for men, three convents for women and a hospice for pilgrims.

However, Jerome himself lived in a cave near the birthplace of Jesus, where he labored for 34 years on many learned works, the most famous of which was his critical work on the text of Sacred Scripture. This earned for him the title of Doctor of Biblical Science. By the Vulgate, his Latin translation of the Bible, which he completed in 404, by his numerous letters and his treatises on the most varied subjects, he was a living power in the Church. His studies clarified the distinction between which books of the Bible were authentic and which were apocryphal and not to be included in the Bible. Moreover, his commentaries on Scripture have been used down through the ages. Sometimes, his letters provide the only written record of the times in which he lived.

Jerome had a penchant for being in conflict with someone; and it is said that only once did he admit defeat. That was in a debate with St. Augustine on the dispute between Sts. Peter and Paul at Antioch (Gal. 2). But he was a man of intense prayer and great purity of heart, who wore himself out by penance and hard work and died September 30, 420. He was buried near the Church of the Nativity. In the thirteenth century, his body was exhumed and buried in Rome in the Basilica of St. Mary Major.

Jerome and Mary

Jerome loved Mary so much that he built a hospice in Bethlehem so that if Mary and Joseph were to come again looking for shelter, they would have a place to stay. An ardent defender of Mary's perpetual virginity, he wrote a book against Helvidius, who claimed that Mary had other children by St. Joseph after the birth of Christ. He saw virginity consecrated in Mary and presented as proof that on Calvary, the Virgin Son John received the Virgin Mother as a legacy from the Virgin Lord dying on the cross. Because John the Baptist heard the Lord's voice on Mary's lips, Jerome said, he wanted to break out of his mother's womb in order to meet Him.

Prayer

Father, Your priest Jerome so combined spirituality with intellectual activity that both men and women followed him to the land of the Bible. May we, Your people, find in the Scripture which Jerome translated the inspiration needed to fulfill Your great commandments of love. We make our prayer through Christ our Lord. Amen.

Saint John Chrysostom
Doctor of the Eucharist, c.349-407

Conditions in Antioch when John Chrysostom was born there around 349 seemed to augur the struggles which he would endure in later life. Most of the bishops there had Arian tendencies and the Catholics were involved in a divisive schism between two bishops. Baptized in 368, John was ordained a lector three years later. He longed to be a monk and fled to the mountains where he spent six years living as a hermit and studying Scripture. After being ordained a deacon in 381, he spent five years caring for the poor and instructing catechumens. He was ordained a priest in 386 and devoted twelve years to preaching in Antioch and producing the rich literary legacy he left to the Church. So great was his eloquence in explaining Scripture that he was dubbed "Chrysostom" or "Golden-mouthed," and was called the glory of the Christian pulpit.

Made Bishop of Constantinople in 398, John found himself embroiled in ecclesiastical and political intrigue. What Contstantinople wanted was a famous preacher not a reformer, and his effort as well as his style in correcting abuses alienated the clergy, certain wealthy widows, the court and especially the Empress Eudoxia, who considered his corrections as aimed specifically at her. When he refused to grant a church for the Arian Goths, he also incurred their enmity.

In 403, thirty-six bishops convened the Synod of the Oak and leveled forty-six charges against John. Considering the Synod illegal, he refused to appear, was declared deposed and exiled. Recalled shortly thereafter by the Empress, John was again banished and left Constantinople for the last time in 404. While spending three years in Cucusus, he was still honored and loved. Because he continued to be popular and influential through visitors and correspondence, John was destined to be moved farther away into remote Pityus across the Black Sea. Exposed to hazardous conditions, he died in Pontus in 407, as he uttered: "Glory to God for all things."

Few doctors of the Church have left such a rich treasury of writings as John Chrysostom. Among his monastic, ascetical and apologetical treatises is his masterpiece, *On the Priesthood*, extolling the greatness and dignity of the sacerdotal office. His voluminous homilies include about 700 sermons on the Bible alone, in which he stressed morality and personal conversion. His commentaries on the Real Presence have caused John to be called the Doctor of the Eucharist. He also left 236 letters. His writings are said to contain a complete manual of the Christian life.

John Chrysostom and Mary

Commenting on Isaiah 7:14, John Chrysostom pointed out that because "Emmanuel" means "God with us," it gives evidence that God truly took on our human nature and became the Son of Mary. Isaiah was expressing wonder at the Incarnation, he said, and indicated explicitly that the Son of God equal to the Father deigned to be born of a Virgin. Chrysostom called Mary a boundless ocean of mercy and an abyss of the immense perfections of God. Comparing Mary to Eve, he states that: "A virgin drove us from Paradise; through a virgin we have found eternal life." In Eve, the wood of the tree and death were symbols of our defeat, he said, but in Mary, the wood of the Cross and the death of Jesus became symbols of our victory. (O'Carroll, 198)

Prayer

Father, Your servant Saint John Chrysostom left us in his writings a complete manual of the Christian life. Grant that we may be sustained in life's trials by repeating with him, "Glory to God for all things." We ask this through Christ our Lord, Amen.

Saint Ambrose
Doctor of Virginity, c.339-397

No one was more surprised than Ambrose when he was elected Bishop of Milan in 374 A.D. As governor of the Roman province, he was responsible for keeping the peace and was in the act of trying to quell a violent dispute between Catholics and Arians about who should succeed the late Arian Bishop Auxentius, when someone cried out, "Ambrose Bishop." The whole assembly in the crowded basilica then took up the cry and elected him bishop by popular acclaim.

After his election had been approved by Church authorities, Ambrose was ordained bishop eight days later. First of all, he gave all his riches to the Church and to the poor. Then, realizing that his classical Roman education had not prepared him to be a bishop, he set about mastering Sacred Scripture and the writings of the Fathers of the Church.

While Arianism had lost much ground in the West, Milan still remained one of its strongholds. This was due to Auxentius, whom Ambrose replaced. He had been installed as Bishop of Milan by the Emperor Constantius in 355 and had succeeded in remaining there, in spite of the opposition of Saint Hilary of Poitiers. Ambrose then became one of the champions of the faith during a second phase of the Church's fight against Arianism. A zealous defender of Catholic belief in the equality of the Three Divine Persons and the divinity of Christ, Ambrose set about destroying the remnants of this heresy both by his writings and his conflict with the Empress Justina.

Once, when the Empress tried to take over a basilica in Milan for an Arian Church, Ambrose and the faithful barricaded themselves inside it. While under siege there, he composed some of his time-honored hymns for the people to sing and introduced the practice of having psalms and hymns chanted by two alternating choirs, as continues to be done today in the Liturgy of the Hours.

From the day of his election as bishop, Ambrose was heavily involved in political matters and was a close friend of the Emperor Theodosius. But he always upheld the rights of the Church despite serving as a trusted advisor to imperial rulers and carrying out at their request many diplomatic missions. For this reason, Ambrose has sometimes been called the Doctor of the Independence and Unity of the Church. And he gained the title Doctor of Virginity because of the five works devoted to virginity, a subject on which he was the most eloquent.

Ambrose left a priceless legacy of homilies and writings, both pastoral and practical. They were always prepared as occasion demanded and in order to meet some special need. Saint Augustine came to hear Ambrose preach because of his eloquence but eventually was drawn by what he had to say. That led to his conversion and his baptism by Ambrose.

After making the faith attractive for twenty-three years by his gentleness, goodness and moderation, Ambrose died in Milan during Holy Week in 397. He was fondly remembered as "A pearl glistening on the finger of God."

Ambrose and Mary

Devotion to Mary assumed a new significance through the writings of Saint Ambrose. In staunchly defending the truth of the Virgin Birth, he appealed to reason by precedents in the realm of nature as logical proof of God's plan for the Incarnation. He appealed to faith by citing the Scriptures. In his *Commentary on Luke*, he called on all Christians to imitate Mary by stating: "Let Mary's soul be in each of you to proclaim the greatness of the Lord. Let her spirit be in each to rejoice in the Lord. Christ had only one mother in the flesh but we all bring forth Christ in faith."

Prayer

God of joy and love, Your holy bishop Ambrose eased the burdens of his people by means of hymns and psalms. May we learn from his example to face life's difficulties with songs of praise in our hearts. We ask this through Christ our Lord. Amen.

Saint Augustine of Hippo
Doctor of Grace, 354-430

By the end of the fourth century, Christianity had become dominant in the Roman Empire and Arianism had lost its influence. But God had been preparing Augustine to prevent absorption of the Church by the prevailing culture and to refute new heresies of the time. Spending his early life as a God-seeker, it was as a God-finder that he became Bishop of Hippo in 396 and by his remarkable genius and personality laid a foundation of faith which has endured down to the present time.

Born in Tagaste, Numidia, in 354, Augustine showed little promise in his early years that he would supply the basis for Christian tradition in the West. During a hiatus in his education, he fell into a pattern of sensuality which continued until his conversion at age 32. Always a serious student, his search for truth gradually became a journey to Christ. When a university professor in Carthage in 374, his reading of Cicero's *Hortensius* set him on the pursuit of wisdom. Attracted by their claim to teach everything by use of reason and their teaching that only the darkness within caused one to sin, Augustine joined the Manichees but soon abandoned this sect over unsatisfactory answers to his queries.

After teaching in Rome for a year, he obtained a chair as professor in Milan, where he began to listen to St. Ambrose at first for his eloquence and finally for his teaching. Reading certain Platonic books engendered a mystical experience which revealed the spiritual within himself and the utter transcendence of God. This led him to read the Epistles of St. Paul.

Oppressed by the weight of his sinful habits, he went through a moral crisis which came to a head when he heard a child's voice repeating, "Take and read." Picking up the Bible, he read, "Put on the Lord Jesus Christ and make no provision for the flesh." From that moment, all doubt disappeared and he was soon baptized by Saint Ambrose.

"Late have I loved You," Augustine wrote. But in his 43 remaining years, he was chosen by the people of Hippo as their bishop, spoke tirelessly against heresies, left an immense literary heritage in defense of the Catholic faith and clearly formulated the doctrine of the Blessed Trinity. His most famous book, the *Confessions*, shows how lovingly he placed the power of his personality into a brilliant service of the Church. Augustine is placed in the forefront of the Doctors of the Church.

Augustine and Mary

Augustine taught that the relationship between Mary and the Church rests on her virginal motherhood.

Mary's Son made His Spouse, the Church, like His virginal mother. The Church is mother through charity and virgin through integrity of faith, he said. Just as there is a special relationship between Mary and the Church, it also exists between Mary and the members of the Church, who conceive the Eternal Word by faith and engender Him in the minds of others by preaching His word. Augustine compared Jesus and Mary to two mystical harps: "What is sounded on one," he says, "is sounded on the other, even though no one has touched it. When Jesus is in sorrow, Mary is in sorrow; when Jesus was crucified, Mary was crucified."

Prayer

God of love, Your servant Saint Augustine applied the full power of his remarkable personality to the unstinting service of Your Church. May we follow him in seeking our soul's true rest in You. This we ask through Your Son, Christ the Lord. Amen.

Saint Cyril Of Alexandria

Doctor of the Incarnation, c.375-444

At the end of the Long Century, the Wars of the Lord were again engaged with regard to the Person and nature of Christ; and the great doctor, Cyril of Alexandria was sent by Providence to defend the personal unity of Christ. Born in Egypt in the late fourth century, the first firm date in Cyril's life is 403, when he accompanied his uncle Theophilus, patriarch of Alexandria, to attend the Synod of the Oak in Constantinople. He succeeded Theophilus in his see and immediately showed his pugnacious temperament by driving the Jews from Alexandria and closing the churches of the Donatists, who taught that the validity of the sacraments depends on the moral character of the minister. Although he said that he preferred peace, Cyril would not settle for it at the expense of orthodox Church teaching.

Thus, his fearless attack on Nestorianism would gain for him the title of Doctor of the Incarnation. Nestorius, patriarch of Constantinople, claimed that the Son of God, who was perfect from all eternity, could not have had a human birth. In Christ, then, there were two separate persons linked in a relative unity. There were two Sons, one God and one man. Mary could not be called *Theotokos*, Mother of God, but only *Christotokos*, Mother of Christ. This "Two-Sons" theory did away with the Incarnation, undermined the Redemption, since only the human person died for us, and made Communion cannibalism.

Cyril agreed that the only begotten Son of God was perfect before the Incarnation but that He willed to take on Himself a human nature, which in no way changed His divine nature. When the Son of God became flesh and was born a man, no new person was produced by the Incarnation. The Word was born by uniting human nature with the divine nature. Jesus is one Divine Person with two natures, radically united as soul and body are united in the human person. Therefore, Mary is *Theotokos*, Mother of God. Pope Celestine I agreed and delegated Cyril to preside at the Council of Ephesus in 431. Condemned by the Council, Nestorius was deposed and Cyril was instrumental in putting an end to this controversy.

A born theologian and watchful guardian of the true faith, Cyril wrote a book, *Quod Unus Est Christus* (On Correct Belief in Christ) explaining the unity of Christ. He also left many other polemic writings, letters and sermons. Cyril's spirituality is always Christocentric within a Trinitarian framework. He taught that the image of God in the human person is the source of one's dignity and that the restoration of that dignity came through Christ's Incarnation, Resurrection, and Ascension.

Cyril and Mary

Saint Cyril was the greatest protagonist of the Divine Motherhood of Mary. At the Council of Ephesus, he delivered what is rightly called the most famous Marian sermon of antiquity in which he gave Our Lady a series of glowing titles and credited her intercession for all the glories of salvation and sanctification. Preachers and poets have borrowed passages from this homily down through the centuries. Cyril contributed in great degree to the rapid development of devotion to Mary which followed the Council. After Ephesus, her feast days multiplied throughout the Catholic world. Cyril stressed Mary's perpetual virginity and her part in the Redemption.

Prayer

Heavenly Father, You raised up Saint Cyril of Alexandria to defend the human and divine natures in the Person of Your Son. By his prayers, may we come to realize that Jesus became human to make us partakers of the divine. We make our prayer through Christ our Lord. Amen.

Saint Peter Chrysologus
Advocate of Papal Authority, c.400-450

Still another heresy concerning the Person and nature of Christ arose at the end of the Long Century. Involved in refuting it was Saint Peter Chrysologus, who was born around 400 in Imola, Italy, and may have died there in 450. Little is known about his life except what is found in his homilies and in his famous letter to Eutyches, who erred concerning the two natures in Christ. Eutyches, archabbot of a monastery in Constantinople, carried away in refuting the "Two-Sons" heresy, went to the opposite extreme and denied that Christ had a true human nature. Thus, he proposed a "One Son" heresy, called Monophysitism, which claimed that Jesus had only one nature, the divine. The human nature, he maintained, was absorbed in the Divinity as a drop of wine in the ocean.

When Eutyches was deposed and excommunicated by the patriarch of Constantinople, he pleaded with Peter to intervene for him with the Pope. Peter then wrote Eutyches an important letter in which he said, "In the interest of peace and the faith, we cannot judge in matters of the faith without the consent of the Roman bishop." Cyril urged Eutyches to submit to the decision of Pope Leo the Great. At the time, Eutyches was an old man and it has been said that he erred due to ignorance and stubbornness. This letter contributed to the recognition of the primacy of the Bishop of Rome. In 433, Peter became Bishop of Ravenna, which at that time was the capital of the Roman Empire in the West and the residence of the imperial court.

The Empress Gallia Placidia was so impressed with his sermons that she became his patron. Peter left 183 of these discourses which were collected by Felix, who was bishop of Ravenna from 708 to 717. Most of these contain explanations of Scripture for use in the readings of the Liturgy of the Hours. In his sermons, Peter did not seek theological depth or original speculation but stressed moral guidance for daily living. Some sermons were geared toward condemnation of heresy and others were dedicated to praise of Our Lady. Because his sermons present such a firsthand picture of Christian life in Ravenna in the fifth century, they are of great historical value. All of them were very short and were delivered with such eloquence that Peter was called "Chrysologus" or "golden-tongued."

Peter had close relationships with Pope Sixtus III and with his successor, Leo the Great. Unfortunately, Peter Chrysologus died one year before the Council of Chalcedon in which the doctrine of the two natures in one Divine Person was confirmed; but he had made his contribution to the triumph of this truth, which unfortunately was not accepted by the entire Church and brought about schismatic branches of Christendom.

Peter Chrysologus And Mary

Peter lived in the generation extolling the Council of Ephesus which declared Mary *Theotokos*, Mother of God. A Marian theme is found in his five sermons on the Annunciation, his four on the Incarnation, and in his Christmas sermons. Stressing Mary's divine motherhood, Peter says: "She bore Him who bears the world, she brought forth the One who brought her forth, she fed Him who gives food to all living things." Insisting on her virginity, Peter wrote: "The Virgin conceives, the Virgin brings forth, the Virgin remains thus." He was the first among the Latins to speak of Mary as Spouse of God through whom God, in the shelter of her womb, looked forward to the salvation of the lost, life to the dead and a relationship between the earthly and those in heaven. (O'Carroll, 284)

Prayer

God of goodness and love, Your bishop Peter Chrysologus left us a legacy of moral guidance for daily living. Grant that we may follow his teaching in carrying out Your will moment by moment. We make our prayer through Jesus, Your Son. Amen.

Saint Leo The Great

Doctor of the Unity of the Church,
c.400-461

One of only two Popes called "The Great," Leo I is deemed the greatest Pope of Christian antiquity, because in a time of political and ecclesiastical turmoil, he was capable of effecting Christian unity under the supreme authority of the successor of St. Peter. Born in Tuscany, Italy, around 400, Leo served as deacon to both Pope Celestine I and St. Sixtus III, whom he succeeded in 440. He began his pontificate by delivering ninety-six sermons against the heresies of the times.

Outstanding among his writings was his *Tome to Flavian*, the patriarch of Constantinople, at the height of the "One-Son" controversy. After Flavian had deposed Eutyches, Dioscurus, who had succeeded St. Cyril as bishop of Alexandria, prevailed upon the Emperor Theodosius to summon a council which met at Ephesus in 449. Eutyches was acquitted of heresy and reinstated in his office, while Flavian and other bishops were deposed. When Pope Leo the Great heard this, he dubbed the council a "Robber Synod," and called a general council at Chalcedon in 451. The nearly six hundred bishops who attended heard the *Tome to Flavian*, which clearly stated the doctrine of the two natures in Christ. They all rose and exclaimed, "That is the faith of the Fathers; that is the faith of the Apostles! So we believe! Peter has spoken through Leo!" That statement reflected one of Leo's central policies—to bring the Church under the jurisdiction of Rome, the see of St. Peter.

He firmly believed that everything he did and said as Pope in governing the Church was participated in by Christ, head of the Mystical Body, and concurred in by Peter, in whose place he acted. Thus, he insisted on

liturgical, canonical and pastoral uniformity. Because
of his concept of the divine nature of his mission and
the rights it supposed, he saw Rome as the center of
unity in the Church.

While Leo's sermons show him to be a true pastor
and a moralist teaching free will and individual effort,
his 173 letters, which are all official, show him as a
man of authority acting by simple but fearless faith,
as taught in the Gospels. Leo stressed that Christ and
the Church do not exist in the past but that we see what
the Apostles saw and touch what they touched. In 452,
Leo dissuaded Attila the Hun from sacking Rome. No
longer did the prestige of the Church derive from the
Empire after Leo's time. He died in Rome in 461.

Leo the Great and Mary

In defending the two natures in Christ, Leo affirmed
Mary's real motherhood and her perpetual virginity. He
said: "In the whole and perfect nature of true man, true
God was born, complete in His own, complete in ours...
He was conceived by the Holy Spirit in the womb of the
Virgin Mother who brought Him forth with her virginity
intact, as she had conceived Him in preserving it." By
assigning a saving role to the Incarnation, Leo enhanced
Mary's part in it and states that there is no hope of
salvation for humankind unless the Virgin's Son was His
Mother's Creator. Leo summarized his teaching in the
Canon of the Mass by placing Mary first: "In union with
the whole Church, we honor Mary, the ever virgin Mother
of Jesus Christ, our Lord and God." (O'Carroll, 217-8)

Prayer

God of truth and goodness, your servant Saint Leo
the Great always acted in concert with Christ Your Son
and Peter, His vicar on earth. May Your Church be able
to maintain the unity which Leo established under the
primacy of the Holy Father. Grant this through Our Lord
Jesus Christ, Your Son, who lives and reigns with You
and the Holy Spirit, one God forever and ever. Amen.

A Walk Through History With
The Doctors of the Church

PART II

The Middle Ages

500 to 1500 A.D.

Saint Gregory The Great

Servant of the Servants of God, c.540-604

The first of the Doctors of the Church in the Middle Ages was Saint Gregory the Great, pope from 590 to 604. Gregory is considered a bridge between the ancient and the medieval world and had great influence on the development of theology and canon law. His works are cited more frequently than those of any other Latin Father of the Church. St. Thomas Aquinas quoted Gregory 374 times in his *Summa Theologica*. He is one of only two popes called Great and earned this title by eminent virtue, his art of governing and his writings.

Born in Rome around 540, Gregory's genius for practical affairs caused him to become prefect of the city in 570. He presided over the Roman Senate and oversaw the food supply, finance and policing of Rome. After his father's death, he turned the family home into a Benedictine monastery and founded six other monasteries in Sicily. Although he remained a monk at heart, he was constantly called upon to settle political matters. As a deacon, he was sent as papal legate to the Byzantine court in Constantinople. Returning to Rome in 586, he served as counselor to Pope Pelagius II and was chosen by popular acclaim to succeed him when Pelagius died from the plague in 590.

One of his first efforts as pope was to conduct a three-day penitential procession throughout Rome to pray for the cessation of the plague. Carrying an image of Our Lady, the procession visited churches on the way and ended at the basilica of St. Mary Major. When the government was indifferent to the incursions of the Lombards, Gregory concluded an agreement with them that saved Rome and caused the people to look on the Pope as their defender. Calling himself the Servant of

the Servants of God, Gregory insisted on the Pope's
universal authority over the Church. He established the
temporal power of the Church by using its patrimony
from extensive property to assist the poor and displaced
families.

Gregory's oratorical works include homilies on the
Scriptures. His moral teaching is found in the *Moralia*,
an exposition on the Book of Job which is a storehouse
of dogma, asceticism and mysticism. His *Pastoral* out-
lines the dignity and duties of the priest; and his
Dialogues treat of the lives of the saints, the immor-
tality of the soul and the four last things. Gregory left
an indelible stamp on the liturgy with his *Sacramentary*,
and Gregorian Chant is named in his honor. Besides
seeking to evangelize the barbarians on the continent,
he sent Saint Augustine of Canterbury to teach the faith
to the Anglo-Saxons in England. Gregory's spirit was
that of a contemplative and he considered his teachings as coming directly from the Holy Spirit. He died
in Rome in 604.

Gregory and Mary

Commenting on 1 Timothy 2:5, Gregory pointed
out that it was as Son of the Father and Son of the
Virgin that Jesus is called the One Mediator between
God and humankind. He made distinctions between the
divine and human natures of Jesus by saying: "He was
from the Father without a mother before the ages, the
same at the end of the ages from a mother without a
(human) father." At Cana, Gregory had Jesus addressing
Mary in these words: "I do not recognize you in (working)
the miracle, which I do not do from the nature I got
from you. When the hour of death will have come, I shall
recognize you as my Mother for it is from you that I
have the power to die." He saw the Incarnation as an
espousal by the Father of the eternal Son with His
human nature in the womb of the Virgin Mary.
(O'Carroll, 159)

Prayer

God of our hearts, Saint Gregory the Great remained a contemplative while faithfully performing mighty deeds for Your Church. Give us the grace to follow his example by practicing a loving docility to the Guest of our hearts. Grant this through Christ our Lord. Amen.

Saint Isidore Of Seville

Guardian of the Liberal Arts, c.560-636

aint Isidore of Seville was not only a contemporary of Saint Gregory the Great but was also his friend and advisor. Born in Cartagena, Spain, around 560, Isidore was raised by his brother, Saint Leander, and his sister, Saint Florentina. Another brother, Saint Fulgentius, became bishop of Cartagena. Isidore himself succeeded his brother Leander as Bishop of Seville about 600 and began an episcopate of thirty-seven years during which he presided over several councils. The most important of these was the Fourth Council of Toledo, which convened in 633 and decreed liturgical uniformity in the rites of the Mass for Spain, the founding of seminaries in all dioceses and a ritual for the chanting of the Divine Office. Isidore proclaimed that only gifted students were to be ordained priests and stressed the obligation of celibacy.

Isidore's chief aim as bishop was to have a renewed and vibrant Church in the heart of what was then the Visigothic kingdom. He also felt that he was called by God to preserve all the secular and religious knowledge that was available in the seventh century. In a time bereft of learning, he sought to rescue all ancient knowledge for his uneducated countrymen. Thus, he produced innumerable works which show his own vast knowledge, his capacity for hard work, his zeal for the good of the Church and his overriding purpose of bringing his people out of the darkness of barbarianism. These writings earned him the reputation of being the most learned man of his time and were used extensively all during the Middle Ages.

Isidore's religious works showed that he considered the Scriptures as divinely inspired; and he added the Book of Revelation to the biblical canon. He explained the great Christological mysteries and provided the first collection of a systematic body of doctrine and pastoral practice. Isidore's historical works reconstructed the history of Spain and gave information on Spanish authors and bishops before the seventh century.

His greatest claim to fame, however, comes from his principal work, the *Etymologiae*, which is a comprehensive encyclopedia of all the liberal arts and their application to the whole gamut of human knowledge. The wealth of information in it became the basis of study, research and instruction by scholars who followed Isidore. This tremendous contribution to human knowledge shows that Isidore was never surpassed as a compiler. He believed that all knowledge must seek God and lead to wisdom.

Isidore died in Seville in 636 after giving tremendous witness of self-emptying and charity in his last days.

Isisdore and Mary

Growing up in Seville, Isidore was part of a faith
community in which devotion to Mary was a way of life,
part and parcel of his nationality and Spanish
patriotism. Such devotion dated back to 40 A.D. when
Our Lady was believed to have appeared to Saint James
the Apostle to encourage his efforts in evangelizing
Spain, a significant event corroborated in the writings
of St. Isidore. When Gregory the Great asked his brother,
St. Leander, to come to Rome to advise him, Isidore was
sent in his place. Upon returning to Seville, he brought
as a gift of the Pope to Leander an image of Mary that
Gregory had long revered in his private oratory. It was
the image which Gregory carried in procession through
the streets of Rome when the plague ceased in 590. This
image is venerated today as Our Lady of Guadalupe in
Caceres, Estramadura, Spain.

Prayer

Lord of all creation, in order to lead souls to You,
Saint Isidore compiled all knowledge existing in his time
and provided spiritual guidance for both clergy and laity.
May we also deepen our prayer lives by following sacred
reading with careful reflection. Grant this through our
Lord Jesus Christ, Your Son, who lives and reigns with
You and the Holy Spirit, one God, forever and ever.
Amen.

Saint Bede the Venerable
Last of the Latin Fathers, c.673-735

enerable Bede is proof that the efforts of Saint Gregory the Great to convert the Anglo-Saxons were successful. He was born near the end of the seventh century around 673 on the lands belonging to the monastery of Sts. Peter and Paul at Wearmouth-Jarrow, England. Brought at an early age to the monastery to be educated, he remained there and lived what appeared to be a quiet life but which culminated in his reputation as the most learned man in Western Europe of his time. He thus succeeded Saint Isidore of Seville in earning this title. Bede is said to have made only two short trips, one to York and the other to Lindisfarne to obtain material for his biography of Saint Cuthbert. But this born scholar used the voluminous monastic library as well as the accounts of reliable eyewitnesses in composing the works which give concrete evidence of his encyclopedic knowledge.

"I have spent the whole of my life," he said, "devoting all my pains to the study of scriptures, and, amid the observance of monastic discipline and the daily task of singing in the Church, it has been my delight to learn or teach or write." His writings which presented both knowledge and the value of knowledge had a major influence on English literature. His scientific works treated of natural phenomena, grammar and his specialty, chronology, in which he furthered the custom of dating years from the Birth of Jesus and the use of A.D.

His *Ecclesiastical History of the English People* is the sole source of much early Saxon history and is one of the most important historical works of the early Middle Ages. Other historical writings were a *History of the Abbots of Wearmouth* and the *Life of St. Cuthbert* in both prose and verse. Bede's theological works include commentaries on Scripture based on the teachings of the Latin Doctors of the Church. He also contributed to English literature with poems, prayers and homilies.

His witness as a monk radiant with holy joy inspired Plummer to write: "We have not, it seems to me, amid all our discoveries, invented as yet anything better than the Christian life Bede lived and the Christian death which he died." Working up to the end, he kept dictating to his last sentence an English translation of the Gospel of John. He then summoned the monks, gave them gifts, asked for their prayers and was laid on the floor where he died on the eve of the Ascension while singing the Gloria with his brethren. In 853, some 118 years after his death in 735, the Council of Aachen bestowed on Saint Bede the title "The Venerable," which he had already enjoyed in his lifetime.

Bede and Mary

Venerable Bede marveled at Mary's humility despite the unparalleled favors which God had showered on her. In saying "He who is mighty has done great things for me," Mary attributed every good gift to God alone. Of this, Bede says: "It is a great thing for the Queen of Angels to be a virgin; it is a great thing for her to be a mother; it is a very great thing for her to be a virgin and Mother of God; but what surpasses all else is that, great as she is, Mary considers herself as if she were nothing." Bede also speaks of the Church as conceiving Christians and giving birth to them without pain just as Mary conceived and brought forth Christ. Both remain virgins even in giving birth through the Holy Spirit, he said.

Prayer

Loving God, Your faithful priest Venerable Bede gifted his companions with profound knowledge and radiant joy. May we also strive to make others happy

by living a life of love. We make our prayer through
Christ Your Son. Amen.

Saint John Damascene
Doctor of the Incarnation c.675-750

aint John, a contemporary of Venerable Bede,
was called Damascene because he was born in
Damascus, Syria, around 675. He also earned
the title of Doctor of the Incarnation, since all his
writings center on Christ. John succeeded his father as
an advisor and tax-collector for the Islamic Caliph who
ruled Damascus but resigned these posts rather then
deny his Christian faith. He then entered St. Sabas
monastery in Jerusalem and led a life of exceptional
virtue and tender devotion to Mary, the Church and the
saints.

Having been ordained by John V, patriarch of
Jerusalem, he taught in the monastery, preached in
Jerusalem, counseled bishops on matters of faith and
produced over 150 works all written under obedience
to his superiors. His writings are inseparably connected
with the campaign of the Church against the Iconoclasts
who sought to destroy all sacred images. John composed
three discourses against the Iconoclasts which contain
the whole theology of the Church concerning the veneration of sacred images.

He taught that it is impossible to picture God but that Christ, Mary, saints and angels, all of whom have appeared in human form, can be pictured. Because venerating these images is not adoration, it is lawful to do so. Teaching that these images lead ultimately to God, John listed advantages of such veneration as teaching divine gifts, nourishing piety and serving as instruments in receiving graces from God.

His most important work was the *Fountain of Wisdom*, which included a history of heresies and a comprehensive exposition of the Christian faith. Considered as one of the most important works of the end of the patristic era, this book contained one hundred chapters dealing with God, creation, the destiny of humankind, Christology, salvation and the four last things—death, judgment, heaven, and hell.

Because of his eloquence, his homilies earned him the title of Golden Speaker. Many of his sermons dealt with praise of the saints, the sufferings of the martyrs and the mysteries of the liturgy. John was also a poet and wrote a number of hymns chiefly to celebrate the principal feasts of Jesus.

John lived a very busy life. Although he is renowned for fighting heresy, he also cultivated great virtue and was a humble, obedient monk. He was declared a saint by the faithful even before his death. The last of the Greek fathers, John gained great influence by trying to compile the whole of patristic teaching rather than by promulgating new ideas. He died near Jerusalem around 750.

John Damascene and Mary

"O Lady...today we offer ourselves to you; to you we consecrate our mind, soul, body, in a word, ourselves entirely, and with psalms, hymns, spiritual canticles, we honor you with all our power." These words of John unquestionably witness to his tender love for Mary. A great proponent of her Assumption, he delivered three of his greatest homilies on this feast day at the site of Mary's dormition near Gethsemane. He also preached a sermon on Mary's nativity in the Sanctuary of the Sheep Pool, which is said to have been the place of her birth. John thought the word *"Theotokos"* (Mother of God) expressed the whole mystery of the Incarnation because the true God was born of Mary. (O'Carroll, 200)

Prayer

Lord God, by his defense of the true faith, Saint John Damascene gained the title of Doctor of the Incarnation. May we follow his example in focusing our lives on Christ, Your Son. We ask this in the name of Jesus. Amen.

Saint Peter Damian
Reformer and Diplomat, 1007-1072

Peter Damian was considered one of the strongest personalities of the eleventh century and one of the greatest servants of the Church whose influence was felt in many areas, religious and political. He was born in Ravenna, Italy, in 1007. One biographer says that he had a very harsh childhood and worked as a swineherd for one of his brothers. Another brother named Damian recognized Peter's gifts and had him educated in Ravenna, Parma, Modena and

Faenza. After a brief teaching career and ordination, he entered the Benedictines at Fonte Avellana in 1035. Being elected prior in 1043, Peter was able to model his monastic life after the manner in which he believed it had been organized originally by Saint Benedict.

Later he progressed from seeking reform among the Benedictines to the larger challenge of correcting abuses in the Church. In 1051, he wrote a treatise dedicated to Pope St. Leo IX, which attacked abuses among the clergy such as concubinage and simony. Two years later, he wrote another significant reform treatise on the legitimacy of simoniac ordinations. After being appointed Cardinal Archbishop of Ostia in 1057, Peter undertook reform more vigorously in virtue of his office. Looking on these efforts as a joint venture of the Church and the Empire, he fulfilled many missions for the Popes and rulers. In 1068, he traveled to Mainz in the hope of stabilizing the marriage of King Henry IV and his wife, Bertha. His efforts to promote more rigorous discipline throughout the Church covered nearly a quarter of a century and were always pastoral and practical.

Peter is outstanding among medieval writers in the number and range of his works. He left the Church a rich treasure of letters, sermons, lives of the saints, epigrams, prayers, hymns and poems as well as liturgical and scriptural writings. He found his inspiration in Scripture, the Fathers of the Church and Latin literature. Peter is credited with learning how to reconcile the active with the contemplative life.

He is said to have added Damian to his name in gratitude to his brother, who believed in his potential. After having made one last journey for the Pope in order to bring about closer ties between Rome and his native city of Ravenna, Peter died at a monastery in Faenza in 1072. Devotion to him rose spontaneously from the people.

Peter Damian and Mary

Peter Damian excelled as a preacher on the Blessed
Virgin at a time which was characterized by a great
upsurge in devotion to Mary. Peter speaks of Mary as
the door of Paradise and the ladder of heaven, which
joins the depths of earth to the heights. Mary, he said,
opened heaven to us, since life lost by humanity is
restored through her. He taught that the same Body
of Christ which Mary brought forth is the Body we
perceive on the altar during the Eucharistic Celebration.
Peter also composed an office of Our Lady for daily use.
He said that it would have been impossible for the
redemption to take place unless the Son of God was born
of Mary. (O'Carroll 285-6)

Prayer

Lord, Saint Peter Damian employed both pastoral
and practical means of ridding Your Church of abuses.
May we continue to use both prayer and action in
advancing the holiness of Your people. We ask this in
Jesus' Name. Amen.

Saint Anselm Of Canterbury
Father of Scholasticism, 1033-1109

The eleventh and early twelfth centuries saw the emergence of another great light in the history of the Church. Saint Anselm, called the Father of Scholasticism, is considered to be the most important writer from Augustine to Thomas Aquinas. Born in Aosta, Italy, he went to France to study and entered the Benedictine monastery at Bec in 1060. After being made abbot in 1078, he visited England regularly to oversee affiliated monasteries there. In 1087, William the Conqueror sent for Anselm to visit him on his deathbed. While in England in 1093, he was appointed Archbishop of Canterbury by popular acclaim and was consecrated the next year. But as a strong advocate of the rights of the Church, he refused to accept the pallium from King William Rufus, who took possession of the See of Canterbury when Anselm went to Rome.

While in Italy, Anselm attended the Council of Bari, where he defended the dogma that the Holy Spirit proceeds from both the Father and the Son. After King Rufus died in a hunting accident in 1100, Anselm was recalled to England by the new King Henry I, who subsequently demanded that Anselm take an oath of allegiance to the king. When Anselm refused, the king asked him to go to Rome. After three years, King Henry renounced the right of the throne to invest bishops by means of ring and crosier; and the Church was thus freed from royal politics. Anselm then returned to England in 1106 and in service to the king acted as regent of the nation while Henry was in Normandy in 1108.

Anselm sought to prove articles of faith by reason alone. If Scripture and proofs from reason seem to clash, he held that faith prevails. His is the famous saying: "I do not seek to understand in order that I may believe, but I believe in order to understand." In his systematic works, Anselm showed the existence of God as the one Uncaused Cause of everything else. He also clearly presented the doctrine of three Divine Persons of one essence. His main work *Cur Deus Homo* (Why God Became Man) showed that since sin is an infinite offense against God, a God-Man had to atone for it. Anselm's prayers and meditations reveal his deep love of God and his desire to advance daily toward the fullness of joy in His presence. Moreover, his voluminous letters are the most significant source of English Church history during his lifetime and show the richness of his spirituality. Anselm died in Canterbury in 1109.

Anselm and Mary

Anselm's great love for Mary is recorded in *Alloquia Caelestia*, a treatise in her praise. He says: "O, woman admirably unique and uniquely admirable, grant me the grace that your love be constantly in my heart and that you bear me forever within your heart." Her sanctity surpasses that of all other creatures and gains her the dignity of becoming the restorer of the world, Anselm taught. He also believed that her sufferings were greater than those of any of the martyrs and that being raised so high, nothing but God is greater than Mary. Anselm declared that his mind failed him and his tongue was dumb when he wished to contemplate the immensity of Mary's grace and glory. (O'Carroll, 33)

Prayer

God of mystery, Your learned doctor Saint Anselm taught us that understanding of sublime truths follows unshaken faith in them. Through his intercession, may we value faith more than reason and firmly believe in order to understand. Grant this through Christ our Lord. Amen.

Saint Bernard Of Clairvaux
The Mellifluous Doctor, 1090-1153

Gracing the Church near the same period as Anselm was Saint Bernard of Clairvaux, who is called the Last of the Fathers of the Church because of his tremendous influence on the religious, ecclesial and political life of the twelfth century. Called upon by bishops, popes and monarchs to intervene in their affairs, Bernard is said to have governed the churches of the West from his Trappist monastery in Clairvaux, France.

Born in a castle in Burgundy in 1090, he entered the Cistercian Order at Citeaux in 1112 after the death of his mother. Proof of his charismatic personality is the fact that by describing the beauty of religious life in glowing terms, he persuaded thirty companions to enter with him. He restored the Cistercian Order to its original fervor and founded the Abbey of Clairvaux, which became the motherhouse of sixty-eight other monasteries.

Although Bernard had sought monastic solitude, he was called upon to preach, write and travel all over Europe on missions for the Church and the state. In obedience to Pope Eugene III, Bernard preached the Second Crusade proposed by King Louis XI of France when the Holy Places were threatened. A strong defender of the papacy, he helped to avert a schism in the Church when two popes were elected in 1130. As a champion of the faith, he preached against the heresies of Abelard and of the Albigensians, who denied the resurrection of the body. Even near the end of his life, he helped the bishop of Trier to settle a conflict in his diocese. As a man of God assisting in political matters, Bernard was frequently asked by monarchs for advice or to act as an arbitrator in affairs of state. He was so frequently called upon because Bernard is said to have had no rival as a peacemaker whether it was in settling disputes between bishops and clergy, warring cities, or rulers and their subjects.

But Bernard earned the title of Mellifluous Doctor, because he taught a new type of spirituality which introduced such an element of joy and encouragement into the pursuit of union with God that his talks and his writings were considered to be as "sweet as honey." A great exponent of the love of God, Bernard seemed to cast fire on the earth wherever he was. Moreover, miracles seemed to happen everywhere Bernard went because of his preaching. It has been said that since the early days of the Church, there had been no greater miracle worker than Bernard and people came from far and near to be healed of their illnesses.

As a mystic and a saint, Bernard left behind over 500 sermons and 300 letters which continue to touch hearts and witness to the excellence of his life and works. He died at Clairvaux in 1153.

Bernard and Mary

Saint Bernard's love for Jesus was accompanied by a tender devotion to Mary, which inspired the most beautiful of his writings. Altogether, they form a comprehensive treatise on Mariology. Bernard's love of Our Lady centered around her dignity as Mother of God, which entitled her to graces and privileges granted to her alone. He believed that God willed that all blessings come to us through Mary's hands and that our spiritual life flows from her Immaculate Heart. Bernard taught that to love Jesus was to love Mary. He composed the familiar and beautiful prayer, the Memorare.

Prayer

Heavenly Father, Saint Bernard permeated all his teachings with an uplifting element of joy and encour-

agement. Grant that like him we may become true
heralds of Your love and attractiveness. We ask this
through Our Lord Jesus Christ, Your Son, who lives and
reigns with You and the Holy Spirit, One God, forever
and ever. Amen.

Saint Anthony of Padua
The Evangelical Doctor, 1195-1231

irst among the doctors making their
contributions to the Church in the thirteenth
century was Saint Anthony of Padua. He was
born in Lisbon, Portugal, in 1195, and in a very short but
extraordinary life of thirty-six years earned many titles,
such as Hammer of Heretics, Wonder Worker and Living
Ark of the Covenant. After becoming an Augustinian at
the age of 15, Anthony was serving as a guest master
when a group of Franciscan Friars arrived on their way
to serve as missionaries in Morocco. After they were
martyred there, their relics were returned to Lisbon, and
Anthony was inspired to continue their mission. He then
took the Franciscan habit in the presence of his
Augustinian brothers in Coimbra in 1220. He was sent
to Morocco as a missionary but became violently ill. On
the return trip, his boat was driven off course and
landed in Sicily. From there he went to Italy and
participated in the famous Franciscan Chapter of Mats
in 1221.

Quite unknown among his new brothers, Anthony's extraordinary gift for preaching was discovered when he was called upon to speak without preparation before a distinguished gathering of Franciscans and Dominicans. Commissioned to preach in Italy and France, Anthony became known as the Hammer of Heretics, because wherever he preached, souls were reconciled to the Church. Combining zeal with eloquence, Anthony converted many of the Cathars and Albigensians. In 1230, Pope Gregory IX asked him to put aside all other duties and concentrate on preaching. By his daily sermons in Padua, he reformed the city, abolished a debtors' prison and aided the poor. So great was his veneration as a preacher that it was said to have surpassed that of his patron, Saint Antony of Egypt.

Moreover, Saint Anthony's reputation as a Wonder Worker was widely known. At the time of his death, forty-seven proven miracles were on record. They included replacing a severed leg, restoring to life a witness needed to testify in a murder case and the power of bilocation. Despite pouring rain, people listening to Anthony did not get wet.

The title of Living Ark of the Testament was bestowed on Anthony by the Pope, because of his knowledge of the Bible. He had already become an expert in Sacred Scripture while an Augustinian and studying at Santa Cruz in Coimbra, Portugal. Saint Francis of Assisi made Anthony the first theologian of his order that he might serve as an inspired interpreter of Sacred Scripture for his Franciscan brothers. Pope Gregory IX called Anthony "Teacher of the Church and Evangelical Doctor."

Anthony's holiness was so apparent that on hearing of his death, the people of Padua took to the streets and cried out: "The Saint is dead." Over thirty years after his death, Anthony's tongue was found to be as red and fresh as it had been in life.

Anthony and Mary

Anthony learned to love Mary in his mother's arms. She offered him to God at Our Lady's shrine in the Lisbon cathedral and often repeated the name of Mary to him. Since he believed firmly in the Assumption of Mary, he refrained from reading a passage in the Office that seemed to throw doubt on it. Mary then appeared to him and assured him that her body was taken up into heaven three days after her death. When violently tempted, Anthony called on Mary. At the end of his life despite weakness, Anthony found voice to call out: "0, Glorious Lady," to pay final tribute to Mary who had watched over him all his life.

Prayer

God of power and might, You gave Saint Anthony extraordinary gifts enabling him to work wonders and convert many to the faith. May we imitate him in using the power of Your word to bring others to union with You. Grant this through Your Son, our Lord Jesus Christ, in the unity of the Holy Spirit. Amen.

Saint Albert the Great
The Universal Doctor, c.,1200-1280

The lives of the three illustrious doctors prominent later in the thirteenth century were closely interconnected. The first of these was Saint Albert the Great, a Dominican bishop, philosopher and patron of scientists. He was called "Great" even in his lifetime because of his vast knowledge in all fields of learning and is known as the Universal Doctor in view of his immense contributions to medieval theology and scholastic philosophy. A Bavarian born in Lauingen, Germany, around 1200, Albert went to Padua to study and joined the Order of Preachers there. Being sent to Paris around 1241, Albert delighted in discovering the "New Aristotle," recently translated. It was also in Paris that he met the other doctors-to-be, Thomas Aquinas and Bonaventure.

Since nature and grace were in complete harmony in his perception of God's plan for creation, Albert embraced Aristotle's explanation of the absolute unity of body and soul and perceived the study of nature as worthy of pursuit in its own right. He saw this approach to the physical world as using human knowledge to search divine mysteries, to investigate the causes at work in nature, and to demonstrate that there is no conflict between reason and faith.

At the request of his students, Albert began a monumental exposition of the whole gamut of human knowledge based on the works of Aristotle. In this work of twenty years, he is said to have described "the entire cosmos from stones to stars." One of his students, Ulric of Strassburg, said that Albert was "a man so superior in every science that he can fittingly be called the wonder and miracle of our time."

When he returned to Cologne in 1248 to direct the studies of young Dominicans, his student Thomas Aquinas accompanied him. In 1253, Albert was elected provincial of the German Dominicans. In 1256, Albert, Thomas Aquinas, and Bonaventure went to the papal curia in Anagni to defend the Dominicans and Franciscans, the so-called Mendicant Orders, from the attacks of William of Saint-Amour and others.

Ordered by Pope Alexander IV to become bishop of Ratisbon in 1260, Albert corrected the abuses there in two years and then resigned. But he was later recalled by Pope Urban IV to preach the Crusade throughout Germany and Bohemia. While he was on his way to the Council of Lyons in 1274, he heard of the death of Saint Thomas Aquinas and exclaimed, "The light of the Church is gone." After a life of unreserved consecration to God and unflagging search for wisdom and virtue, Albert went to Paris in 1277 to defend the works of Thomas, his renowned student. He died a holy death in 1280.

Albert and Mary

Kneeling before the image of Mary, Albert heard her say, "Leave the world and enter the Dominicans." When discouraged about difficulty in learning and tempted to leave, Mary appeared to him, consoled him and granted his request for comprehensive knowledge of human learning. His writings on Mary's prerogatives surpassed any written before. In his book, *Mariale*, he described her physical beauty, her exceptional intellectual powers and her perfection in virtue—all of which she enjoyed as the Tabernacle of God. Overflowing with love of Mary, Albert wrote hymns in her honor and sang them while walking. He said that to prepare to serve the Son, one must first serve His Mother.

Prayer

Creator God, Source of all being, You enabled Saint Albert to reconcile faith and reason, nature and grace. May the wonders of Your creation also lead us to greater knowledge and love of You. We ask this through Our Lord Jesus Christ, Your Son, who lives and reigns with You and the Holy Spirit, one God, forever and ever. Amen.

Saint Thomas Aquinas
The Angelic Doctor, 1225-1274

hen Thomas Aquinas, St. Albert's best student, was born in Roccasecca, Italy, in 1225, his parents had great plans for him. They wanted him to become the abbot of the monastery at nearby Monte Cassino and presented him there as an oblate when he was about six years old. His interest in theology was apparent early on as was shown by his frequent question, "What is God?" The God about whom he wondered had other plans for Thomas. When the monks were ejected from Monte Cassino, he studied at the University of Naples where he was attracted by the Dominican way of life and joined the Order of Preachers at age 19. At their mother's bidding, his brothers pursued Thomas as far as Rome and took him home where for a whole year they tried unsuccessfully to get him to return to Monte Cassino.

In 1245, after his family freed him, Thomas began to study in Paris under Saint Albert the Great, who recognized his genius and took him to Cologne where he was ordained. In 1252, he was sent back to Paris to study for a doctorate in theology and to teach. At this time, Thomas began a long period of illustrious productivity, which has caused him to be ranked with Saint Paul and Saint Augustine as one of the greatest theologians in the history of the Church.

Early in his Paris tenure, he collaborated with St. Bonaventure and St. Albert in defending the Dominicans and Franciscans against the secular clergy, who sought to take away teaching positions from members of religious orders. In 1259, Thomas was summoned to Rome to serve Alexander IV and the two popes who succeeded him. Up to 1268, he was theologian of the Holy See and was able to do thorough research on the Fathers of the Church and Aristotle. During this time, he began the *Summa Theologica*, his masterpiece, which made theology a science. It synthesized theology with Aristotelian philosophy and reconciled faith and reason. The *Summa* and his other works encompass virtually all of Catholic doctrine.

In 1272, he began organizing a Dominican school in Naples and drew immense crowds to his lectures, as he had done in Paris. Eventually, his continuous labors caused illness and exhaustion. Nevertheless, he complied with the summons of Pope Gregory X to attend the Council of Lyons in 1274. The hardships of the journey caused Thomas to collapse on the way; and he died at the Cistercian Abbey in Fossa Nuova on March 7. His holy death and the subsequent miracles worked through his intercession caused him to be venerated as a saint in a very short time.

Thomas Aquinas and Mary

Thomas had a deep and heartfelt personal devotion to Our Lady. Writing at length on her Divine Motherhood, he explained that as Jesus is only one Divine Person, Mary can truly be called the Mother of God. This unparalleled grace placed her above the angels and saints because of the fullness of grace that was hers; and it gave her "a kind of infinite dignity from the infinite good which is God," Thomas wrote. He also saw Mary as the representative of all humanity, who brought about a spiritual marriage between the Son of God and the whole human race. He believed that in every danger or need, we can find refuge in this glorious Virgin. (O'Carroll, 343-4)

Prayer

God of truth, Saint Thomas Aquinas desired only Yourself as the reward for his profound writings about You. May we, like Thomas, be preserved from intellectual pride and follow the way of the meek and humble Jesus. We ask this through Christ Our Lord. Amen.

Saint Bonaventure
The Seraphic Doctor, c.1217-1274

 aint Bonaventure, who received his doctorate in Paris along with Saint Thomas Aquinas, was drawn to the Franciscans early in his life when he was cured of a critical illness through the intercession of Saint Francis of Assisi. Born around 1217 in Viterbo, Italy, he studied in Paris with the Franciscan, Alexander of Hales, and entered the Friars Minor around 1243. Elected Franciscan minister general in 1257, he revised the constitutions of the Order and offered the Friars a viable adaptation of poverty so faithful to the ideals of Francis that he is considered the second founder of the Franciscans.

When word came that he was appointed cardinal-archbishop of Albano, Bonaventure is said to have been washing dishes and asked the papal legates to hang the red hat on a nearby tree branch until he had finished his task. Then he went to meet Pope Gregory X at Mugello, north of Florence, and traveled with him to Lyons, France, where the Second Council of Lyons was to take place. Here he was consecrated bishop in November, 1273. Bonaventure then helped the Pope to prepare for the Council which opened May 7, 1274. He preached and presided over several meetings in the effort to resolve differences between the Greek and Roman delegates. Then, while involved in Council affairs, Bonaventure died suddenly July 15, 1274 and was buried in the Franciscan church in the presence of the Pope and assembly.

Even though Bonaventure was deeply engaged in administrative and pastoral concerns, he left a rich legacy of significant works. In all of his writings, his aim was to help souls to progress in the way of love; and his work has left an enduring mark on Christian spirituality down through the ages. One of his most important works is *The Soul's Road to God*, in which the reader's thoughts are raised step by step to union with God. His treatise, called *On the Threefold Way*, became a classic formula of spiritual literature as the soul is led from the *purgative* to the *illuminative* to the *unitive* stage of the ascent to God. Bonaventure is said to have become a mystic earning the title "Seraphic Doctor" by entering deeply into the inner life of Saint Francis while writing his *Legend of St. Francis*. He stirred all of Europe by his burning desire to draw all people to a higher life.

Bonaventure and Mary

After reading Bonaventure's poetic account of Mary's visit to Elizabeth, it is easy to see why he was the first to introduce the Feast of the Visitation. Not only did he catalogue her unique privileges in his writings, but he brought her to life by inviting his readers to "hear the Virgin singing for joy." He called Mary an immense vessel of grace, since she became powerful through and with the God she encompassed within her. God could not have made her a more perfect mother, he said, since He could not have given her a more excellent Son. Bonaventure marveled at Mary's poverty and especially at her humility, since she called herself a poor handmaid, despite having been called full of grace, overshadowed by the Holy Spirit, made the Mother of God, and appointed sovereign Lady of heaven and earth.

Prayer

Eternal God, Your servant Saint Bonaventure saw the entire universe and all human history as revolving around You. May we in turn realize more deeply that You are the center of our lives. We ask this through Christ the Lord. Amen.

Saint Catherine of Siena
Spiritual Mother and Papal Advisor, c.1347-1380

Adding luster to the Church in the fourteenth century was Saint Catherine, who was born in Siena as one of the twenty-five children of the Benincasa family. She was such a joyful child that she was called Euphrosyne, the Greek word for joy. At the early age of six, she had her first mystical experience and committed herself to virginity at age seven. When her mother insisted that she marry, her father intervened and gave her a room for meditation and prayer. At 16, she became a Dominican tertiary and spent the next three years in seclusion and penance. In 1368, she had a vision in which Christ revealed that He had accepted her as His bride and wanted her to carry His love to the world.

Catherine then began to draw a nucleus of friends and disciples who called her Mother and whom she considered as family. For their spiritual instruction, she began to write what eventually became a voluminous production of letters, which later on would have a significant influence on public affairs. When she aggressively supported Gregory XI's Crusade against the Turks, Catherine was summoned to Florence to appear before the Dominican General Chapter of Affairs and was cleared of any wrong doing. Providentially, the Chapter appointed Raymond of Capua as spiritual director of Catherine and her followers.

During the next four years from 1374 to 1378, Catherine had her greatest impact on events in society. Her efforts to halt the war of Florence against the papacy ended in failure; but she was successful in persuading Pope Gregory XI to bring the curia back to

Rome from Avignon. In 1375, she went to Pisa in behalf of the Crusade. While there, she had an ecstasy and received the stigmata.

Returning to Siena, she devoted herself to writing her *Dialogue*, her spiritual testament, while she grieved over the schism in the Church due to the election of an anti-Pope. At the request of Pope Urban VI, Catherine was in Rome from 1378 until her death in order to give the Pope counsel and endeavor to gain support for him as the rightful successor of St. Peter. In agony over the state of the Church, Catherine offered herself as a victim for ending the schism. After this, she suffered a stroke and died in Rome in 1380 while surrounded by her followers who had come to Rome with her. She was buried in the Church of the Minerva in the Holy City.

Catherine ranks high among mystics and spiritual writers. Hers is a Christ-centered spirituality that stresses the love of God symbolized by the Blood of Christ. Her *Dialogue* and nearly four hundred letters addressed to kings, Popes, bishops, men and women religious, civic leaders and private individuals are said to have given her a place in Italian literature beside Dante and Petrarch.

Catherine and Mary

After Catherine learned the Hail Mary at age 5, it became her constant prayer. She begged Mary that she might belong to Jesus alone; and at her mystical marriage, Our Lady presented her to Jesus and asked Him to espouse her. Constantly referring to Our Lady as "Sweet Mary," she also gave her many other titles, such as, Temple of the Trinity, Minister of Mercy, Ocean of Peace, Vessel of Humility and Fiery Chariot. Mary, she said, carries and spreads the fire of love because her Son is love. In every circumstance, Catherine saw Mary as an exemplar and a secure refuge. She wished to lead everyone to Our Lady that all might surrender to divine intimacy. All of her letters were dedicated to the same "Sweet Mary."

Prayer

Lord God, Your virgin Catherine of Siena, made a total offering of herself for the welfare of Your Church. Following her example, may we also strive to meet its needs by prayer, penance, holiness and action. We make our prayer through Christ our Lord. Amen.

A Walk Through History With
The Doctors of the Church

PART III

Post-Reformation

Defenders of the Faith

Sixteenth and Seventeenth Centuries

Saint Peter Canisius
Second Apostle of Germany, 1521-1597

Saint Peter Canisius was one of three Doctors of the Church who played key roles in enabling the Church not only to survive the Protestant Revolt but to emerge from it rejuvenated and prepared to meet future challenges. Marching at the head of Catholic forces in Germany, Peter Canisius used every means at his disposal to save as much of the German empire as possible for the Catholic faith. Born in the Netherlands in 1521, he was the eighth Jesuit to take vows in this new order. He taught in the first Jesuit school in Messina, Italy, and wrote *The Fathers of the Church*, the first book ever published by a Jesuit.

Assigned to Germany in 1549, Peter was so effective in counteracting the Protestant Revolt for the next three decades that Pope Leo XIII called him the Second Apostle of Germany after Saint Boniface. Jesuit colleges proved to be Peter's most powerful resource in combating Protestantism, which was making severe inroads into the Church in Germany. Appointed by Saint Ignatius as the first Jesuit provincial in Germany in 1556, Peter Canisius developed the three already existing colleges in Ingolstadt, Vienna, and Prague and established new ones in Munich, Innsbruck, Dillingen, Tyrnau and Hall. He also concentrated on the all-important reform needed within the Church and is credited with revitalizing the faith in both Germany and Austria, which were in grave danger of being lost to the reformers.

One way in which Peter exerted the greatest influence within the Church was by writing three catechisms for the instruction of the faithful. The little catechism, including fifty-nine questions and answers, was meant for children and those being instructed. A *Minor Catechism* was written for youth; and his greatest catechism, called *Summa of Christian Doctrine* was considered the most important writing of the Catholic Reformation with the exception of the *Spiritual Exercises* of Saint Ignatius. Its 213 questions and answers were meant for university scholars. So important were the catechisms that they underwent 200 editions in Peter's lifetime alone. Thus, his name and "catechism" became synonymous.

It has been said that every office Peter filled, every college he founded, every letter he wrote were directed toward the same end—the growth of staunch faith among Catholics. Each of these he undertook with unfailing zeal and self-forgetfulness. Peter died in Fribourg, Switzerland, where he had been transferred to oversee the Jesuit college. To the end in 1597, he continued to preach and to write.

Peter Canisius and Mary

True to his major role in the Counter-Reformation, Peter Canisius undertook the first defense of Mary against the reformers. In his *Summa*, the most scholarly catechism, he outlined the traditional teaching on the Mother of God. Then he wrote a comprehensive work called *Of Mary, the Incomparable Virgin*, which included the writings of ninety Fathers and Doctors, 4,000 biblical texts and more than 10,000 references to patristic and scholastic theologians. It outlined Mary's perfect life, her perpetual virginity, her honor as Mother of God, her Assumption and the devotion shown her by the Church. It also explained certain biblical texts which if misinterpreted could bring dishonor to Mary. (O'Carroll, 282-3)

Prayer

All-powerful and ever-living God, to revitalize the faith after the Reformation, Saint Peter Canisius provided solid education for children, youth and adults.

May Your Church keep alive the same zeal for imparting that knowledge that leads to love. We ask this through Christ the Lord. Amen

Saint Robert Bellarmine
Champion of Church and State Relations, 1542-1621

orn near Florence, Italy, in 1542, Robert Bellarmine was destined to become one of the greatest of the Jesuit apologists who played leading roles in the Catholic Reformation. After studying at the Jesuit college in his native town, Robert entered the Society of Jesus in 1560 and was cited as the outstanding student of his class in the Order's Roman College. Ordained in Louvain in 1570, he was the first Jesuit to teach theology at the University there and he preached with such deep spirituality and intellectual prowess that Protestants from England would come over to hear him. Many of them were converted.

Convinced that superior theological training was necessary to defend Catholic doctrine against the Reformers, Robert undertook serious study of Scripture, Church history and the works of the Fathers of the Church in order to systematize Catholic teaching. While at Louvain, he also wrote a Hebrew grammar for his students.

In 1576, he was appointed as professor at the Roman College to prepare English and German seminarians. His lectures delivered over a period of eleven years were compiled in a vast synthesis called the *Controversies* in which Robert compared the errors of the reformers with the teaching of Catholic theologians. He did this in a positive way by pointing out both the strengths and weaknesses of the Protestant position. So important was this great work that twenty editions were issued in Robert's lifetime. It was used for several centuries after his death as the most complete defense of the Catholic faith which the Church possessed.

In 1588, Robert was appointed as spiritual director at the Roman College. His instructions culminated in the compilation of two catechisms, one for children and another for teachers. Two years later, he found his writings a mixed blessing when Pope Sixtus V decided to place the first volume of the *Controversies* on the Index because, it stated that papal authority in temporal matters is not immediate and direct. The sudden death of Sixtus prevented this from happening and Robert was exonerated.

Robert then served as rector of the Roman College, provincial of the Jesuits' Neapolitan province and theologian to Pope Clement VIII, who made him a cardinal and appointed him Archbishop of Capua. In 1605, he was recalled to Rome by Pope Paul V to serve the universal Church.

Robert had written a treatise entitled *On the Art of Dying Well* and showed that he had learned that lesson. When informed that his own death was imminent in 1621, he called that good news. His body rests in the Church of Saint Ignatius in Rome.

Robert Bellarmine and Mary

Robert stated that Mary was the first to take a vow of virginity. He linked the Immaculate Conception with Mary's election by God, who in choosing her before all others, preserved her from original sin and adorned her with incomparable graces. Commenting on Mary's presence on Calvary, Robert stressed her union with Jesus by the most perfect maternal love. Despite her profound sorrow and her love for her Son, she loved the honor of the Father and the salvation of the world more. After the Ascension, Robert wrote, Mary taught and consoled the faithful. He cited miracles around the world as proof of how efficacious it is to invoke her. (O'Carroll 73-4)

Prayer

God of the living and the dead, in promoting the Catholic Reformation, Saint Robert Bellarmine compiled the most complete defense of the faith known in his time. Grant that we may so live our faith that, like Robert, we can welcome our death as good news. We make our prayer through Christ the Lord. Amen.

Saint Lawrence of Brindisi
Capuchin, polemicist, diplomat, 1559-1619

The efforts of Saint Lawrence in the Post-Reformation era caused Pope Benedict XV to say that he earned "a truly distinguished place among the most outstanding men ever raised up by Divine Providence to assist the Church in time of distress." He exercised tremendous influence at this time as an eminent preacher, defender of the faith, religious superior and diplomat.

Born in Brindisi, Italy, in 1559, Lawrence studied in Venice and joined the Capuchin Franciscans there at the age of 16. Ordained in 1582, he began to use his mastery of many languages and the fruits of biblical scholarship in preaching against Protestanism in northern Italy and beyond the Alps in Bohemia, Austria and Germany.

Since he was nearly always a major superior of the Capuchin Order, he was able to establish priories in many countries; and the Order became one of the main forces of the Catholic Restoration. Lawrence, when superior general, would walk to visit the nearly 9,000 Capuchins in 34 provinces located in Italy, France, Switzerland and Spain.

He was often called upon by civil authorities to serve as a diplomat. Emperor Rudolf appointed him as chief chaplain to the Christian army in 1601; and he went before the disheartened forces as he held up a cross and urged the men to advance in order to turn back the Moslems from Hungary. In 1610 he was asked to use his remarkable diplomatic skills in persuading King Philip III of Spain to join the Catholic League. He also served as papal nuncio to the royal court of Bavaria, Germany, until 1618, when he retired to a monastery in Caserta, Italy. Called out of retirement to undertake a mission to King Philip III on behalf of the people of Naples, the journey ended with his death in Lisbon, Portugal, in 1619.

Lawrence left a rich legacy of writings. His *Omnia Opera* contains fifteen tomes, eleven of which contain sermons that demonstrate his holiness and his brilliance. His hearers attested to his remarkable eloquence in delivery; and his fluency in many languages enabled him to bring many people back to the Church. His writings refuting Lutheranism are important for firsthand information about Luther's personal life and teachings. Among his scriptural commentaries, his *Explanation of Genesis* gives a clear exposition of the first eleven chapters of *The Book of Genesis* and presents strong evidence of his expertise as a Biblical scholar.

Lawrence and Mary

Evidence of his tender devotion to Our Lady is given in the eighty-four sermons which Lawrence delivered before vast audiences in order to motivate people to honor Mary. In these homilies, he praised her Immaculate Conception, her Assumption and her other prerogatives in an inimitable manner. In her praise, Lawrence used the Bible, tradition, the writings of the Fathers and the liturgy. In multiplying her titles, Lawrence said: "She has become the daughter of God the Father, the true Mother of God the Son, the spouse and unique comfort of the Holy Spirit, the Queen of Heaven, the mistress of angels, the empress of the universe." Indeed, the writings of Lawrence on Mary comprise a complete treatise on Mariology.

Prayer

Lord of the ages, Saint Lawrence of Brindisi was a staunch defender of the faith after the Reformation. Grant that, like him, we may meet the challenges which the Church faces in our times. We ask this through Our Lord Jesus Christ, Your Son. Amen.

A Walk Through History With
The Doctors of the Church

PART IV

Doctors of the

Great Love of God

Sixteenth through Nineteenth Centuries

Saint Teresa of Avila

Doctor of Prayer, 1515-1582

The five remaining Doctors of the Church concentrated more on union with God than defense of the faith. The first of these is Saint Teresa of Avila, who is classified as a mystic, that is, a person in love with God. But she was certainly not in an ecstasy all the time. Rather, she possessed remarkable good sense in dealing with reality.

Born in Avila in 1515, Teresa entered the Carmelites there at the age of twenty. She found that the convent in her home town was somewhat lax in observing poverty and the enclosure. Thus, she lived quite an indifferent life for her first twenty years as a Carmelite. But, in 1555, she received an overpowering grace at the sight of an image of Jesus sorely wounded during His Passion. "I felt so keenly aware of how poorly I had thanked Him for those wounds that it seems to me, my heart broke," she said. That religious experience along with reading the *Confessions* of Saint Augustine changed her life and motivated her to work towards the reform of Carmel by observance of the primitive rule, the practice of absolute poverty and the pursuit of an intense prayer life.

Teresa began her reform with herself and quickly entered into a higher degree of perfection. When other sisters wanted to join her, she had recourse to her family to obtain a house where she could institute the reforms. Four sisters took vows in the Convent of St. Joseph in 1562. Many other foundations followed; and in 1568, she inspired Saint John of the Cross to head a reform monastery for men. Both Teresa and John suffered strong opposition, until Pope Gregory XIII allowed a separation of the Discalced Carmelites, who followed the primitive rule, and the Calced Carmelites, who chose not to do so.

Teresa earned the title Doctor of Prayer by teaching perfect prayer not only to her sisters but also to spiritual directors and confessors, who urged her to record her experiences in order to teach many people the way to greater union with God. Her writings have become classics of spiritual literature. In her *Autobiography*, Teresa compares the different stages of prayer to ways of getting water to irrigate a garden. In the *Way of Perfection*, she used the Lord's Prayer as a vehicle for teaching prayer at greater depth. The *Interior Castle* has been called "a divine story of divine love." It entails a journey through various mansions of the castle to the center where the Trinity dwells, since attaining union with God leads a soul to the center of itself.

Suffering to the end, Teresa was expelled from a convent just a few weeks before her death by her own niece. When she died at Salamanca in 1582, she closed a life that combined mystical contemplation with incredible activity, which Teresa had managed with good humor and unfailing common sense. She was proclaimed the first woman Doctor of the Church in 1970.

Teresa and Mary

When Teresa was fifteen her mother died. She begged Mary to become her mother. She looked on Carmel as Mary's order. When she was not accepted as prioress of a monastery, Teresa told the nuns that Mary occupied that office. She told those who helped Carmel that they were helping Mary. She opened her book, *The Foundations*, with these words: "I begin in the name of the Lord and of the glorious Virgin whose habit I wear." Near the end of her life, she said: "Now, like the old man Simeon, I can say, 'I have seen in the order of the Virgin what I desired.'" Teresa considered Mary a special gift of God to her. (O'Carroll, 337)

Prayer

God of love, Your daughter Saint Teresa of Avila was led to total self-giving by viewing an image of Your Son, sorely wounded in His passion. May the contemplation of Christ's sufferings and death also draw us to deeper union with You. We make our prayer through Jesus, the Suffering Servant. Amen.

Saint John of the Cross
Doctor of Mystical Theology, 1542-1591

Like Saint Teresa, Saint John of the Cross, was able to balance a life of contemplation with that of a very active administrator and reformer. Born in Old Seville in 1542, John lived in extreme poverty as a child and had his early education in a home for poor children in Medina del Campo. At age 17, he found work in a hospital owned by Don Alonso Alvarez, who helped him attend the local Jesuit college and later paid for his seminary education. In 1563, John joined the Carmelites in Medina; and after making vows, he studied at the University of Salamanca.

Returning to Medina to celebrate his First Mass following his ordination in 1567, he met Saint Teresa, who told him of her plan to reform the Carmelite order. John, who also had found Carmel lax, wanted to join the Carthusians, but Teresa persuaded him to remain in the order and to join her in her reforms. Thus, with two other men, he founded the first monastery of the Discalced Carmelites and followed the primitive rule in Duruelo in the year 1568. At that time, he took the name of John of the Cross.

His new name proved to be prophetic, since although the reform grew rapidly at first, it later met strong opposition; and a chapter was held in 1575 to put an end to its expansion. Because John refused to conform, he was imprisoned by his own brethren. Able to escape in 1578, he brought about the separation of the Order into Calced and Discalced Carmelites. Because of continuing controversy about the reform, John was banished to a solitary monastery in southern Spain. He died in 1591 in Ubeda, where he had gone for treatment of his leg.

John's writings provide a sublime guide for anyone seeking to pursue a perfect life. He begins the *Ascent of Mount Carmel* by stating that its purpose was to explain how one reaches a high state of perfection. In this book, John shows that the journey of faith requires depriving oneself of anything contradicting full conformity to God and that the senses are to be used solely for God's honor and glory. *The Dark Night of the Soul* is a treatise which explains how God purifies the soul for union with Him; and John's *Spiritual Canticle* is a loving colloquy between the soul and Jesus. Finally, *The Living Flame of Love* treats of a deeper and more perfect kind of love for God. John also left letters, maxims, counsels and about ten short poems with similar themes.

John of the Cross and Mary

John credited Mary with divine favors he had received in life. He said that she had saved him from drowning as a child, had led him to enter Carmel, and had delivered him from prison. In his greatest trials, he found that remembering her favors and looking at her images restored peace to his troubled soul. John emphasized her consent to the Incarnation, her divine motherhood, and the honor which is due to her. John said that he died happy in the thought that he would be able to recite Our Lady's Matins in heaven. As he died, a last request was to be clothed once again in the "habit of the Virgin," which lay beside his bed and which he had worn with such devotion. (O'Carroll, 199)

Prayer

God of love and mercy, Saint John of the Cross endured great trials in seeking to implement his lofty vision of religious life. Grant that like John, we also may be true to Your call in our state of life. We make our prayer through Christ our Lord. Amen.

Saint Francis de Sales
Evangelist and Spiritual Father, 1567-1622

Another Doctor of the Church born in the sixteenth century was Saint Francis de Sales. Centuries ahead of his time, he anticipated Vatican II's teaching on the universal call to holiness. In his day, the spiritual life seemed to have been relegated to the cloisters. Francis sought it out and brought it back to the world to revive devotion among the laity. His masterpiece, *An Introduction to a Devout Life*, showed how every type of life could be sanctified and set forth a spirituality compatible with life in the world.

The eldest of thirteen children, Francis was born in Savoy, France, in 1567 and pursued his education in Annecy, Paris and Padua, where at age 24, he received a doctorate in civil and Church law. At the time of his ordination in 1593, the Catholic religion was suppressed in Savoy. When Duke Charles Emmanuel got control, he asked for volunteers to revive the faith. Francis and his cousin Louis worked in Chablais where they went from village to village preaching, contacting Catholics and trying to make converts.

Finding this approach unsuccessful, Francis began writing a weekly short article on some doctrine of the Church and debating Calvinists whenever he could. When some prominent officials returned to the Church, the number of converts increased. People were drawn by the magnetism of Francis's holiness and his gentle manner. The final result of the four years he spent in Chablais was the acceptance of the faith by the majority of the populace.

In 1599, Francis was appointed coadjutor bishop of the Diocese of Geneva but was not consecrated until 1602. Since he was unable to establish a seminary in the diocese, he undertook the education of priests himself. He held diocesan synods on the Roman rite of administering the Sacraments, wrote a work on hearing confessions and conducted pre-ordination examinations in order to accept only worthy candidates as priests. Religious instruction was given every Sunday and holy day by catechists who belonged to a confraternity. As bishop, he watched over his flock carefully, remedied disorders, and nurtured the people in faith and piety.

Only a few of his 4,000 sermons are extant, but he is said to have been a preacher of conviction and charm as both a father and a teacher. His *Introduction to a*

Devout Life immediately became a classic and might be called his *Summa* of spiritual direction for the laity. His other masterpiece, *The Treatise on the Love of God*, was written for people advanced in perfection and is connected with his founding of the Order of the Visitation in collaboration with Saint Jane Frances de Chantal. Francis intended for this order to be one in which charity and gentleness would rule. His keywords were sweetness and graciousness. Francis died in Lyons on December 28, 1622, after suffering a cerebral hemorrhage.

Francis and Mary

The deep love Francis had for Mary is evident in his desire to have a group of religious who would practice the virtues of Mary visiting Elizabeth. Thus, humility, piety, and mutual charity were to be the hallmarks of the Order of the Visitation. Francis lauded Mary in twenty of his published sermons which were delivered on feasts of Our Lady. He pictured Mary as a creature so holy and united with her Son that no one could love the Son without loving the Mother. Francis saw the Immaculate Conception as a benefit Mary received from the Redemption. He called Mary the Queen of Heaven and said that her Divine Motherhood makes her intercession more powerful than that of any of the saints.

Prayer

Loving Father, by showing that every type of life can be sanctified, Saint Francis de Sales led people to holiness. By his prayers, may we also follow his teachings and respond with all our hearts to God's call to union with Him. We make our prayer through Christ Your Son. Amen.

Saint Alphonsus Liguori
Founder of the Redemptorists, 1696-1787

lphonsus was a contemplative in action. Vowing never to waste a moment, he wrote over one hundred moral, spiritual, and dogmatic works. These writings as well as his musical, artistic, and poetic gifts were all geared to preaching the Gospel especially to the poorest and most neglected. His spiritual writings recalled the great message of God's love so powerfully that they infused a new youth into the Church.

Born near Naples in 1696, Alphonsus had earned a double doctorate in civil and canon law at the university there at age 16. Having lost an important court case, he renounced a legal career and joined Oratorian confraternities to do apostolic work. In 1726, he was ordained a diocesan priest and devoted himself to giving missions and hearing confessions. Shocked by the spiritual abandonment of the poor mountaineers along the Amalfi coast, he began to instruct them. Eventually, he founded a new missionary society of men, the Congregation of the Most Holy Redeemer in 1732. After a slow start, by 1747 it had thirty-six members notable for their closeness to the people, their kindness in the confessional and their clear, straightforward preaching.

In 1762, Alphonsus reluctantly became bishop of St. Agatha of the Goths, where he found 30,000 uninstructed men and women and 400 indifferent priests. He wasted no time in reforming the clergy and religious, establishing programs to assist the poor and providing missions conducted by his Redemptorists. Stricken by a serious illness which left him a cripple, he submitted his resignation and retired to Pagani. Here he was duped into signing a rule imposed by the King of Naples, which differed so much from the original Redemptorist rule that Pope Benedict XIV revoked the canonical status of the congregation except for houses in the Papal States. Unfortunately, Alphonsus died before the two branches of his congregation were reunited.

The influence of Saint Alphonsus was deeply and widely felt. His *Moral Theology*, written for pastoral use, had great impact and qualified him as patron of moralists. His writings contributed to the definition of the dogmas of the Immaculate Conception and papal infallibility. His teaching that God wills the salvation of everyone dealt Jansenism a fatal blow. The theme of his spiritual works is the revelation of God's love for humanity. In his writings on the mysteries of Christ, it is always the love of Christ and the duty to return that love that are stressed. Means to obtain holiness, according to Alphonsus, are the Sacraments and prayer; and the object of prayer is again the love of God. Perseverance in that love would merit the grace of praying without ceasing. His book, *Visits to the Blessed Sacrament*, was a best seller and went through forty editions in his lifetime.

Alphonsus Liguori and Mary

Alphonsus never wrote a letter or book, composed a single prayer or preached a sermon without referring to Mary. He spent seventeen years on his book, *The Glories of Mary*, which is one of the greatest works of Mariology. Our Lady is said to have appeared to Alphonsus many times. Once 4,000 people to whom he was preaching saw a beam of light from an image of Mary on the altar cross the church and strike the face of Alphonsus. The severe physical, mental and spiritual anguish he suffered in his last years was alleviated by the thought of Mary's constant care of him. The night before he died, Alphonsus asked for her picture, kissed it, spoke softly and smiled radiantly. He died the next day as the noon Angelus began to ring.

Prayer

Faithful God, in order to serve You with his whole heart, Saint Alphonsus resolved never to waste a minute of time. Through his prayers, we ask the grace to treasure each moment as it comes and to use it for Your honor and glory. Grant this through Christ our Lord. Amen.

Saint Thérèse Of Lisieux

The Little Flower of Jesus, 1873-1897

Nearly a century after the death of Saint Alphonsus, Saint Thérèse of Lisieux was born in Alençon, France, in 1873. The latest saint to be named a Doctor and the third woman to receive that title, Thérèse led such a hidden life that it seems miraculous that anything at all is known about her. She entered a Carmelite convent in Lisieux at 15, never left it and died at 24. So ordinary had her life appeared that some of her sisters in religion wondered what could be found to write about in her obituary.

Yet devotion to St. Thérèse of the Child Jesus, after her death in 1897, spread around the world at a phenomenal rate, because her autobiography, *The Story of a Soul*, showed that God comes to us in the ordinary and that we find the way to become saints in the small things of everyday. Her so-called "Little Way" is one of trust, love and self-surrender that appealed to the great and the lowly.

Born as the youngest of nine children into a holy and affectionate family, Thérèse entered a winter of trial when her mother died when she was only four. Her idyllic childhood shattered, she became extremely sensitive, shy and withdrawn and when the family moved to Lisieux, she was unable to adjust at a Benedictine abbey school. In 1883, she had a strange illness but was instantly cured when she prayed to Our Lady of Victory. On Christmas in 1886, Thérèse received a special grace which cured her of her excessive sensitivity and enabled her to reach a new maturity and self-possession in which her love of God could flourish. Although since the age of three, she had never refused God anything, she now entered a new stage of intense spiritual development.

After two of her sisters had entered the Carmelite convent in Lisieux, Thérèse sought the local bishop's permission to follow them when she was fifteen years of age. Not being encouraged by the bishop, she presented her request to Pope Leo XIII when on a pilgrimage to Rome. The Pope told her that she would enter if God so willed it. And God did.

In the Carmel of Lisieux, Thérèse found the right atmosphere for her Little Way to come to fruition. Things were far from serene in this convent; but Thérèse joined no faction and concentrated on refusing God no sacrifice in a myriad of small, unspectacular ways, day by day. She believed that her call was to love, since love encompassed every vocation and all virtues.

Thérèse said that she would spend her heaven doing good upon earth; and one obvious proof that she has kept her promise is that *The Story of a Soul*, which became a classic immediately after her death, continues to draw others to intimacy with God. Her advice to a relative on how to become a saint was very simple: "Seek to please Jesus."

Thérèse And Mary

Thérèse's ideal of spiritual childhood led to recognition of Mary as her exemplar. She remembered being miraculously cured when the statue of Our Lady of Victory in her room moved toward her and smiled. On the day of her First Holy Communion, Thérèse made an act of consecration to Our Lady; and her last poem was entitled "Why I Love Mary." During the final months of her short life when she was suffering intensely, she spoke frequently of Mary. As she prepared for death, her eyes looked constantly on two pictures of Mary and on the statue of Our Lady of Victory which was in her room. Her last work on earth was making two crowns from corn flowers in order to please Mary, her mother. (O'Carroll, 343)

Prayer

Holy God, Saint Thérèse of Lisieux inspired the great and the lowly to become saints through the ordinary things of everyday life. Help us to follow her Little Way by seeking to please You in everything we do. We make our prayer through Your Son, our Lord Jesus Christ, who lives and reigns with You and the Holy Spirit, one God, forever and ever. Amen.

BIBLIOGRAPHY
Acknowledgments

Grateful acknowledgment for permission to incorporate copyrighted material is made to Michael O'Carroll, C.S.Sp., for references on how the Doctors honored Mary from *Theotokos: A Theological Encyclopedia of the Blessed Virgin Mary*, Michael Glazier, Inc., Wilmington, Del., 1982, as cited on pp. 5, 7, 9, 12, 15, 17, 22, 32, 34, 37, 45, 47, 49, 59, 67, 70, 75, 78, 85; and to Bishop Donald W. Wuerl for use of the concept and importance of the Long Century found in *Fathers of the Church*, Daughters of St. Paul, Boston. 1982, as seen on pp. iii, vi, vii, and 1.

Other Sources

Allardyce, Isabel. *Historic Shrines of Spain*. New York: Franciscan Missionary Press, 1912.

Athanasius, St. *Life of Antony* and *The Letter to Marcellinus*. Translated by Robert Gregg. *The Classics of Western Spirituality*. New York: Paulist Press, 1980.

Augustine, St. *Selected Writings. Classics of Western Spirituality*. New York: Paulist Press, 1984.

Barr, Robert, S.J. *Main Currents of Early Christian Thought*. New York: Paulist Press, 1966.

Basil, St. *Letters*. Translated by Agnes Clare Way, C.D.P. *The Fathers of the Church*. New York: The Fathers of the Church, Inc., 1947.

Bonaventure, St. *The Soul's Journey into God and The Tree of Life*. Translated by Ewert Cousins. *Classics of Western Spirituality*. New York: Paulist Press, 1978.

Bouyer, Louis. *The Spirituality of the New Testament and the Fathers*. New York: Desclee Company, 1963.

Catherine of Siena, St. *The Dialogue*. Translated by Suzanne Noffke, O.P. *The Classics of Western Spirituality*. New York: Paulist Press, 1980.

Cayre, F. *Manual of Patrology*, Vols. I and II. Paris: Desclee Company, 1940.

Daughters of St. Paul. *The Church's Amazing Story*. Boston: The Daughters of St. Paul, 1969.

Gregory the Great, St. *Dialogues*. Translated by Odo John Zimmerman, O.S.B. *The Fathers of the Church*. New York: The Fathers of the Church, Inc., 1959.

Harney, Martin, S.J. *The Catholic Church through the Ages*. Boston: The Daughters of St. Paul, 1980.

Jerome, St. *Selected Letters of St. Jerome*. Translated by F. A. Wright. New York: G. P. Putnam's Sons, 1933.

John of the Cross, St. *The Collected Works of St. John of the Cross*. Translated by Kieran Kavanaugh, O.C.D. and Otilio Rodriguez, O.C.D. Washington, D.C.: Institute of Carmelite Studies, 1973.

Laux, John. *Church History*. New York: Benziger Brothers, 1936.

McBride, Alfred. *The Story of the Church*. Cincinnati: St. Anthony Messenger Press, 1983.

Merton, Thomas. *The Last of the Fathers*. New York: Harcourt & Brace Company, 1954.

Neill, Thomas P. and Schmandt, Raymond H. *History of the Catholic Church*, Second Edition. Milwaukee: The Bruce Publishing Company, 1965.